FLOWER ARRANGING

For every day and special occasions

By the Editors of

Better Homes and Gardens

An appealingly old-fashioned bouquet   A mixed bouquet in an old ironstone pitcher recalls our Colonial days

Table of Contents

Tulips and lilacs that convey to us springtime's always-new message

Like a poem to spring is this composition of tulips and lilacs. Arranged in the Oriental manner, our flower study reminds us of a bed of tulips abloom beneath a lilac bush, its branches heavy with fragrant lavender plumes. Gracefully flowing lines interpret nature's ways. Subtle, delicate color shadings entrance the eye

Introduction

Something remarkable has been happening all over America during the past decade or two. The art of flower arranging, by no means a new one historically, has subtly captured the imagination of people who formerly took but a passing interest in it.

It is in response—and tribute—to this awakened and growing enthusiasm for a practical as well as visual art form that *everyone* can enjoy and afford that we are pleased to publish this volume—the first that we have issued on the subject.

The art is centuries old

You have only to look at pictures of the most ancient art of China or Egypt, for example, to see that flower arranging has been practiced with truly consummate skill for a great many centuries.

What is *new* today about flower arranging is that it's no longer an art form whose practice is limited to the privileged few. Anyone who has a small garden or access to a florist's shop can share in its pleasures with no need to expend any large sum of money.

Nor should we fail to say that the observing eye of the flower arranger will also discover delightful materials for compositions in the commonest of weeds and grasses that grow everywhere along the roadside.

If we were asked to choose the one trait that seems to us most characteristic of flower arrangers, we'd say it is their ability to recognize beauty in unexpected places.

To the uninitiated, a rock is a rock, and a shell a shell. But to the arranger, they are treasures one can use to enhance the beauty of the flowers and foliage with which they are imaginatively combined.

Garden clubs deserve high praise

Certainly the major credit for setting the example and showing the way to gain pleasure from flower arranging by the amateur should go to the women of the garden clubs all over the world. They have sponsored flower shows and encouraged talented members to demonstrate artistic ways of combining nature's gifts which have been a source of inspiration to countless numbers of people. They have set standards of excellence for both arranging and judging that are everywhere respected and followed.

We salute, also, the members of the florists' profession. Twelve months of the year —in and out of normal growing seasons— do they stand ready to supply us with flowers and foliage for our delight.

Tell your florist of your interest in flower arranging. He will respond enthusiastically and be happy to supply you with "a few of this" and "a little of that" because you are a fellow enthusiast for the joys and rewards of flower arranging.

Beauty has a practical side

In the pages of this book are gathered some of the most beautiful and artful flower compositions we could possibly find. Some are lavish; others are ingenious in making a few flowers look like many. We know you are going to enjoy just browsing through the colorful array in the same way you enjoy a stroll through a picture gallery.

But we have not forgotten the practical side of this art. You will also find tips on keeping flowers fresh longer; suggestions on the equipment to use; step-by-step instructions on assembling many different styles of arrangements; and a great deal else in the way of helpful information. Here's as much as you'll need to know about the art of flower arranging to make your home more attractive all during the year.

We who have had a hand in the preparation of this book are excited about it. We believe you will find it both inspiring and useful, whether you're a beginner or an expert. We feel certain that you will grow in your skill and appreciation of the art of flower arranging as you use it in the years to come.

The Editors
Better Homes and Gardens

Chapter 1

Bring beauty into your home

When you enter a house and are greeted by the sight of fresh flowers attractively arranged, you know at once you're in a home where beauty and hospitality are important.

The familiar phrase—"say it with flowers" —is meaningful because flowers *do* say special things for which it's often difficult, perhaps impossible, to find the right words.

Everyone likes flowers on the table. They please the eye, help to whet the appetite, say that this meal is a special event.

Flowers are good decorators

More and more people are coming to understand the great decorative assets of flowers throughout the home. The splash of vivid color in a bouquet can light up a room. Gracefully arranged foliage can soften and improve severe architectural lines.

There's also a personal reward in selecting and arranging just the flowers that will do most to add to the beauty of your home.

So many of the things in the world about us are necessarily mass-produced. But when you arrange flowers, you alone have selected and placed them in a design that's uniquely yours. To all who seek a creative outlet, it is surely a satisfying activity.

Anyone can learn this art

The art of flower arranging is an easy one to learn. Anyone who loves flowers and growing things—and will take time to combine them with discernment—can succeed in this art.

What makes the bouquet across the page so effective? It's partly that the cool, white contrast of the flowers sharpens the appeal of a warm pumpkin-and-gold background. And it's also the way they're arranged—with an opulent air that suits their setting.

Pictures and ideas in this book will help you to work with flowers, to touch them with magic, to bring fresh beauty into your home.

Elements of design in arrangements

There are almost no "rules" that must be obeyed by flower arrangers. But there are some principles of good design you'll want to be aware of as aids to your own sense of taste and to your self-confidence.

Some happy few are born with so sure a feel for design that they put flowers together artistically without ever consciously following any principles of composition.

But most of us grow in skill as we understand the fundamentals of design and apply them to our flower arrangements.

On these pages we include sketches and simple diagrams to help you see the major elements that add up to good design.

Once you are aware of them, you'll feel freer to follow your own sense of taste as you create designs with flowers.

Proportion

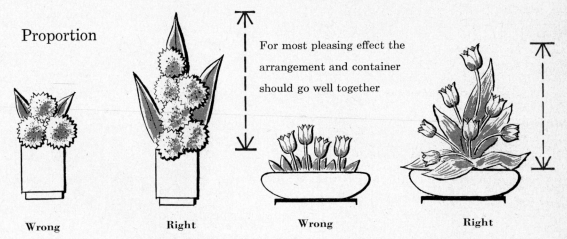

For most pleasing effect the arrangement and container should go well together

Wrong   **Right**   **Wrong**   **Right**

Your flower arrangement is in good proportion when it seems the right size for its container. If you're using a tall vase, the safe, general rule is to have height of flower materials that extend above its rim equal to 1½- to 2-times height of vase

Standard height rule for arrangements in low containers is that tallest stem equal 1½- to 2-times length or diameter of bowl. Experts in Modern and Traditional styles ignore these "rules" as their skill and sense of proportion become well developed

Balance

We say flower arrangements look well balanced when they give us a sense of stability—do not appear to be lopsided.

The two kinds of balance we may seek are: *symmetrical* (two halves are identical or nearly identical); and the *asymmetrical* (two halves are not actually equal but appear to our eyes to have equal weight or importance).

Symmetrical balance is relatively easy to secure. Asymmetrical balance requires greater practice, but can be more rewarding and challenging to our skill.

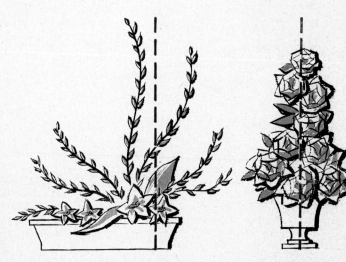

Asymmetrical balance   **Symmetrical balance**

Seek contrasts of color, texture, form—or all three—to avoid monotony

Include *contrast* if you want more interesting arrangements. Combine rough with smooth, dark with light, round and spear

Smooth texture   **Coarse texture**

Contrasting textures in an arrangement are easy to secure. Often you need only take advantage of nature's contrasts—soft, velvety flower petals with shiny, glossy foliage; or coarse, ruffled petals with sleek leaves. When plant material you're using has no "built-in" contrast, use your imagination to make combinations that will offer good textural contrast

Color contrast within a flower arrangement is gained by combining hues of greater and lesser *values*. Pale hues have less value than deep shades. Dark colors will look best low in an arrangement, as they appear heavier to the eye. For help on choosing flowers to make the right color contrast within a room scheme, see the section on color which begins on page 40

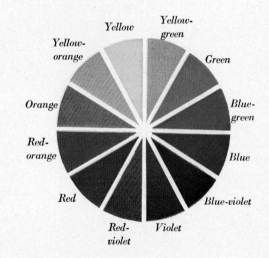

Round shape   **Spear shape**

Contrasting forms, like the rounded bloom and pointed leaf sketched at left, enhance each other when placed together. Deeply cut leaves are more interesting if combined with solid-looking flower heads. Often, a flower's own foliage will supply sufficient contrast. If not, search for others that give the contrast you want

Arrangements are harmonious when all elements are well blended

Harmony or unity is always your final goal in arranging flowers. It is a result of making a skillful selection of plant materials, container, accessories, and setting so that they all seem to belong together. If all these elements are effectively blended, the outcome will be satisfying in design and a harmonious whole

Here are the basic shapes

When you begin with a design in your mind, your flower arrangement is bound to be more successful than if you have no plan.

All arrangements except the Oriental tend to take one or another of the shapes illustrated on these pages. Next time you are arranging flowers, select one of them as your pattern, and vary so it will suit your needs.

Factors that determine your choice of a flower design are: the place you intend to put the arrangement (in a corner, on a dining table, and so forth); size and shape of container you want to use; size and shape of the flowers and foliage you're working with.

The triangle lends itself to many variations in height, width

The triangle is a popular basic shape for symmetrical arrangements of both Traditional and Modern styles. First step is to establish height and width with foliage and flowers. Fill in center with largest blooms ◄

The completeness of the circular shape satisfies the viewer's eye

Nature must love the round or circular form since the majority of flowers do fall into that shape. Arranging them in circular design adds a pleasing element of repetition. Avoid monotony by using foliage that will offer contrast to the dominant round forms ➤

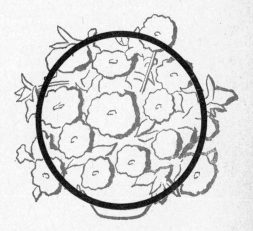

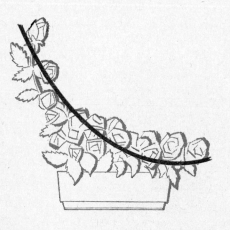

Aimed at sophisticated tastes, the crescent has true appeal

The crescent shape is asymmetrical and an essentially sophisticated design. Before attempting a crescent-shaped arrangement, be sure stems of plant materials you're using are pliable enough to permit manipulation ◄

There's rhythm in a Hogarth curve

The English artist Hogarth once added a palette with an S-curve like the one below to his signature on a self-portrait, with the words "the line of beauty." This serpentine shape is a favorite for flower show entries

The line of beauty

Use torch arrangements to get height

The perpendicular line is often just what you need when you have limited display space. Some glads and their own spear-shaped foliage are excellent for arrangements of this type, but many tall plant materials are equally adaptable

The convex curve is a favorite shape for dining-room-table centerpieces

A convex curve is a good line to follow when designing flowers for the table. It does not need to be tall to be effective, and when it's kept low won't interfere with across-the-table talk or view. It's also attractive from every angle

Face your triangle right or left, depending on location

Flower arrangements which conform in shape to a right-angle triangle are extremely popular with Modern arrangers because of the attractive asymmetry they make possible.

Face the triangle to left or right (as in the two sketches we show) according to the room location you've selected for the completed design.

If the arrangement is to be seen from both sides, remember to turn it around as you work, making sure that each view is as attractive to the eye as the other.

Right-angle triangle arrangements are usually most effective in shallow rectangular containers. Use a needlepoint holder to secure stems.

Three styles of flower arranging

Leading artists in the field of flower arranging—like artists in any medium—are apt to prefer one style of arrangement to all others, depending on personal taste.

But to most of us, each style—Traditional, Oriental, and Modern—has its own charm. We enjoy experimenting with all three, depending on our mood of the moment and the type of flowers and foliage available to us.

Basic to Oriental style is emphasis upon *line* in every design. Traditional style is at an almost opposite pole, achieving its most splendid effects with a *mass* of bloom. Modern, the most recently developed of the three styles, owes more to Oriental than to Traditional in its fascination with line.

We invite you to savor each style in its turn before you choose one as your favorite.

Modern reflects the Oriental use of line

Substitute taste for rules to get at the essence of Modern. Bound by no traditions, this style readily acknowledges an indebtedness to Oriental examples of line designs.

Unlike masters of the Japanese art, Modern arrangers pay small attention to mathematical recipes for the right proportions. The test lies in whether the result appears to have good balance to the sensitive and knowing eye.

This arrangement is typical of Modern in its inclusion of sculpture, driftwood—as well as bird-of-paradise blooms—in arrangement, so they become essential not incidental.

←

Look to the Oriental style for the beauty of simplicity

In every Japanese flower arrangement a triangle is established with flowers or branches. Each element of the triangle is symbolic: the tallest line represents *heaven;* facing and looking to heaven is *man;* looking to both is *earth.*

The arrangement as a whole portrays the ideal harmony that exists between the earthly and the eternal life.

An informal (Nageire) grouping shown at left represents well the Oriental genius for revealing beauty in simplicity.

→

Traditional arrangement is typically full and symmetrical

The influence of Victorian elegance is immediately apparent in this generous bouquet of mixed flowers, arranged in a handsomely decorated china vase.

Arrangers who excel in this style often find inspiration in antique flower calendars and in paintings by the old masters, dating from the sixteenth and seventeenth centuries in Holland, France, and England. It is in the European art tradition that this style has its roots.

1 First step is to place tallest stem — white stock is used here — at center back of holder. Next, insert the shorter stems of lavender stock in front of and at the side of the white stock

2 Long-stemmed yellow roses mark the extreme width of this fan-shaped bouquet, add contrast of form, color. Insert remaining roses of varying stem lengths in front, at sides of stock

→

Our heritage of
traditional
flower arrangement

3 Complete the bouquet with the addition of yellow and white daisies in radiating clusters. Place white ones high, yellow ones low, so they won't be too close to the yellow roses which are of almost exactly the same color.

Arrangements in the Traditional manner call for containers which match style of the bouquet — as this crystal urn does. If the container looks very Modern or Oriental, don't force Traditional designs into it. For a harmonious whole, it is important that all of the elements conform in style.

←

Mrs. Louise B. Fisher, who created all the bouquets pictured on these and the following two pages, is the flower arranger for restored Colonial Williamsburg, in Virginia.

If you've visited there, you have seen the results of her artistry in the flower and fruit arrangements she regularly designs to add fresh beauty to the lovely, old historic rooms.

Keeping alive our Eighteenth Century heritage, Mrs. Fisher has contributed much to American knowledge about Traditional arranging.

Let a flower print be your inspiration

Peonies and iris are the main ingredients of this generously proportioned bouquet which reminds us of antique calendars of flower prints.

In mass arrangements, there's always room for one more flower. Rules are few except that tall, feathery material is almost always used to outline the background, with large, full-blown blooms placed at center.

Step-by-step procedures for a Traditional flower arrangement

1 Select a bowl of generous proportions for this large-scale arrangement. Set into it a square wire-mesh holder. Spread hemlock branches, or other flat greens, at the rear of the holder. These branches should be the tallest materials in the arrangement, establishing height and width of your floral composition.

Place snapdragons—or whatever you are using as the tallest flower material—just in front of hemlock fan.

2 You are ready to begin filling in the arrangement. Hemlock has established the tallest lines of the compositions; snapdragons the next. Material you insert now should not exceed either of them in height.

Cut yellow iris, roses, daisies (or any smaller, more compact blooms of a round form) to assorted lengths. Put them in holder in front of the snaps.

Keep in mind the over-all fan shape of arrangement as you make additions.

3 Add vivid contrast with bright red anemones and a few roses of matching hue. Let a few flowers jut out over lip of container as the eye-catching center of your composition.

Now stand off and see whether there are any "vacant" spots. If so, fill in with yellow carnations or other flowers, wherever they seem needed.

Place a sampling of blooms used in bouquet on table beside arrangement. Use a small cupholder to keep fresh.

The magnificence of many flowers

A generous look is the hallmark of the Traditional manner

In contrast to the Oriental style which has fairly rigid rules about proportions and placement of materials, the Traditional style follows few dictates in these matters.

Usually, the over-all design is fan shaped, and includes a profusion of both flowers and foliage, with a great deal of variety in color and form.

The bouquet pictured at the left is a good example of several distinguishing characteristics of Traditional arrangements: fine, feathery material as background; tall flowers next; smaller, more compact blooms used to fill. There's always "room for one more."

Accessories for Traditional bouquets

Only authentic Eighteenth Century containers are used to hold flowers that grace the colonial rooms of reconstructed Williamsburg. Here are reproductions of a few of the originals: fluted bowls, fingered posy holders, pitchers, jugs, tankards. Containers like them were used in England, brought to America by our colonial forefathers.

It isn't necessary for you to use only authentic reproductions—or true antiques—for Traditional flower arrangements. But the container should be in harmony with the flower composition—whatever its style—if the total composition is to be aesthetically pleasing.

On the shelves with the flower containers are wire-mesh holders in several sizes. They are standard equipment for securing stems of arrangements in the Traditional manner.

The abundant look has strong appeal

When flowers are plentiful, use them generously in mass bouquets

If you have large quantities of flowers available, consider yourself fortunate and be exuberant in your compositions.

Experiment with mass arrangements on a large scale; fashion Traditional compositions which do emphasize quantity as well as quality of flowers.

We show on these pages three ways to create large arrangements using only one type of floral material to a bouquet.

←

This arrangement imitates the breath-taking beauty of an entire tree of flowering dogwood by its fullness. Pruning at the tips of branches gives a lacelike quality to the outer edges of the fan-shaped bouquet

Repetition of form and contrast of textures contributes to a satisfying floral composition

Bouffant bouquet of variegated pink and white carnations is interesting because it concentrates on textural contrasts instead of contrasting forms for effect.

Both flowers and whorl-shaped pittosporum foliage are basically round shapes. Contrast is introduced by the differing textures of soft, frilly flowers against polished-looking foliage.

Additional emphasis of the satin-velvet contrast is given by the glowing patina of the antique silver bowl which has been used as a flower container.

Allowing some of the blooms to extend over the edge of the bowl helps to keep this arrangement from looking too stiff.

→

The brilliance of many red tulips, and the natural sheen of their petals is greatly intensified by the background—a rather somber oil painting whose subject is a bouquet of flowers. The relationship between the living arrangement and the painted one is a matter of style: both of these bouquets are executed in an expansive and Traditional way

Learning the art
of Oriental
arranging

Flowers arranged with loving artistry are constant decorations in Japanese homes. Displayed in a "Tokonoma"—an alcove which is a kind of frame for the flowers and a scroll painting—the arrangement is an indispensable part of an entire way of life.

Guests are made welcome, then brought to sit before the Tokonoma where they will admire the beauty of the flowers for a moment or two of tranquil silence before the ceremonial serving of the tea.

Explore with us the symbolism behind the placement of each flower and stem.

Tomoko Yamamoto, of the Gekha-Soami school, is our Oriental authority and created arrangements on these and next four pages. She was the first woman in Japan honored by the emperor with the title "Flower Master"

Arrangements in Nageire manner aim for simplicity and naturalness

1 Three basic-line flowers in this style arrangement are secured in a triangular placement by needlepoint holder set into basket. Tallest stem is 1½ times over-all height

2 Secondary flowers, mountain and meadow, are set into the triangle formed by the first three stems. All the remaining flowers must be "helpers" which strengthen these elements

Study these diagrams to learn the basic principles of Moribana arrangements

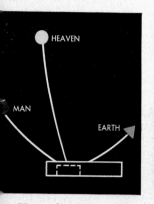

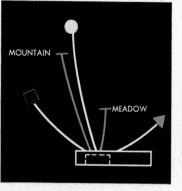

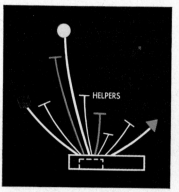

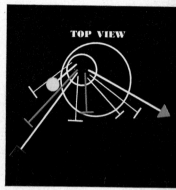

Heaven is 1½ to 2 times container width; man ⅔ height of heaven; earth ⅓ the height of heaven

Mountain, placed slightly behind heaven, adds depth to an arrangement; meadow is placed forward, as lowest point in a composition

Insert helpers to fill in design, but so that they don't conflict with major elements already established; stems must not cross

Top view shows how man and earth lines project forward, at angles, from the main or heaven line

Flower arrangements in the Nageire style typically decorate the tea ceremony

Fable has it that this style of arrangement takes its name from a Sixteenth Century incident involving a famous general, Hideyoshi, and his favorite master of the tea ceremony, Rikyu, in the course of a battle.

The day was hot and a temporary truce was declared to allow opposing generals time to rest and take tea. Rikyu looked about for some flowers —essential to a tea ceremony—and found iris growing nearby.

In lieu of a flower holder, Rikyu thrust his knife through a few flowers and an accompanying leaf, lightly tossed knife and flowers into a container of water, where it landed in an upright position.

Hideyoshi admired the promptness and ingenuity of Rikyu's action and exclaimed: "What a clever throw-in!" From that day on, such arrangements have been called Nageire, the Japanese word meaning a "throw-in."

The story illustrates nicely the emphasis on naturalism—or the simulation of natural growth—which the Nageire style of arranging demands.

1 Flowers should be clamped tightly into holder (see sketch below) with no part of flower, stem, foliage allowed to touch the container. Heaven, man, earth lines should be placed first, in a triangle, with the tip of heaven over center of arrangement

2 In second step, add mountain and meadow. Mountain is cut a little shorter than heaven and is placed slightly behind it, giving depth to the composition. Meadow is low and at center, facing directly front

The type of container sets the style of your arrangement

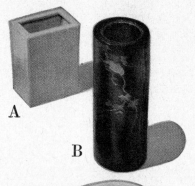

Baskets or type (A) containers are used for "throw-in" Nageire arrangements; tall vases (B) for formal arrangements; shallow containers (C) for informal or Moribana style

3 Further additions, or helpers must follow closely the lines of already placed major elements of arrangement. They should be harmonious in color also. The forked stick-holder at left can, with skill and patience, be whittled by hand. Similar ones, called "kubari" can be purchased ready-made in an assortment of sizes

come first in Oriental arrangements

Love of line is the motivating force behind all styles of Oriental arranging. Unlike the Western attitude which puts flowers first, the style of their arrangement second, the Oriental is primarily concerned with creating a balanced, harmonious composition. Even the humblest of growing things, skillfully arranged, can convey beauty.

One of the great delights, therefore, of an acquaintance with the Oriental style of flower arranging is that it opens new vistas for our enjoyment. Suddenly we can see the essence of beauty in the natural lines of growth, in curve of stem and leaf.

The formal or classical style, in which the roses pictured here are arranged, is the one on which all the more informal styles have been based. Once a form of religious expression, and a part of Buddhist worship, it is used today without religious significance.

HEAVEN

MAN

EARTH

Designs inspired by nature's lines

Every Japanese flower arrangement is, in a sense, a poem in praise of that life force which unites all things under the heavens.

There is no desire to copy precisely any actual form such as one might see in a garden, but rather to pay tribute to the ideal form one sees only in his mind.

Learn from the Japanese to be inspired by nature, to make your expression personal.

Even a single stem—if you choose the right one—can display interesting lines, and actually be a composition in itself. This stalk of lilies, with bud, partly open, and full-blown blooms symbolizes continuing growth in life about us

Garden flowers arranged in informal Nageire style

Gracefully curving stalks of dictamnus are used for the heaven and man positions. Iris leaves, gently manipulated, represent earth line. Iris, with bud on top, to left of and slightly back of heaven line, gives a sense of depth.

The largest purple iris blooms, cut short and facing forward, are the meadow in our nature picture.

Nageire is distinguished from all other Japanese schools of flower arrangement by its characteristic freedom of style. In Nageire arrangements, branches and stems are permitted to cross one another.

Primary emphasis is put upon suggesting natural growth of the plant material, whereas conformity to set rules and artificial curves are of only secondary importance.

Bamboo container is in keeping with informal style of arrangement.

1 Use large needlepoint holder, placed in corner of shallow, rectangular bowl. Prune off undeveloped buds from glad tips. Insert first three glad stems to represent the heaven, man, and earth lines. Consult the Moribana chart on page 21 to help in placing the stems correctly

2 Next add gladiolus to represent mountain and meadow lines. Mountain is a little shorter than heaven, and placed slightly to left and behind it. Meadow is a short stalk, facing forward. It must be the lowest point in your entire arrangement

Moribana style strikes a nice compromise between formal and informal modes

3 To complete this arrangement, four more glad stalks were added, making a total of nine. It is possible to build a smaller arrangement in this manner by using five or seven stalks — or a larger one with 11, 13, 15, and so on. The only rule is that one should use odd rather than even numbers in order to achieve a pleasing and rhythmic effect.

Once the first five stalks have been placed, others are added to fill in the arrangement, without distracting from the total feeling of unity. Practice is the best way to learn when to stop.

The Moribana style, latest to be developed by Japanese flower arrangers, is most popular as a design suited to use in decorating the Western style of home. It combines the naturalism of the Nageire with the formality of the classical school, frequently adds a suggestion of landscape and natural scenery in order to achieve the desired effect.

A shallow bowl, usually of rectangular shape, is the conventional container.

Westerners borrow from Oriental style

To attain an expert knowledge of Japanese flower arrangement, one must be willing to devote years to study and practice. Few Americans have the opportunity—or the desire—to become true masters of the art.

But all of us can learn from the Japanese to recognize the beauty of simplicity. We can borrow from the Orientals their ability to strip away details in order to reveal an essential form which is lovelier than any man-made trimmings or decorations can be.

Applied to flower arranging, the pursuit of simplicity will lead us to look at growing things with a fresh eye. We will learn, too, how to use fewer flowers with larger effect, and how to display flower arrangements in uncluttered surroundings.

On these pages we show you a few examples of American ingenuity at borrowing and translating principles of Oriental art.

Bamboo used in a nature scene

Artful pruning of bamboo silhouettes delicate leaf patterns. Coral formations at the base plus zephyranthes plants on second holder advance a poolside theme in an arrangement by Mirandy

Exotic materials simply displayed

Feathery papyrus dominates a tall arrangement by Mabel Hoyt. Also included are bamboo, ornamental banana blooms, brake ferns, roses, princess flower, snowball and gardenia foliage. The unusual container is actually a Japanese lantern

The setting gives impact to artistic flower arrangements

Learn an effective display technique from the Japanese use of the Tokonoma or wall niche as a "show case" for flower arrangements. Like a frame for a painting, a proper setting increases our appreciation of any artistic creation.

Pictured below is a pleasing Occidental adaptation of a Tokonoma. A gold screen on the grand scale replaces the Oriental alcove and makes an impressive background for a boldly sweeping arrangement of camellia and magnolia foliage, with red amaryllis blooms. Arrangement was designed by Mrs. Joseph Auner.

The Tokonoma is a part of every Japanese home

Distinctive
modern
arrangements
stress line

Mrs. Tommy Bright, who designed the three arrangements shown here, is a regular designer for Florists' Telegraph Delivery; teaches floral design

A trend toward the exotic unites this arrangement and its sophisticated setting

The stark simplicity of many Modern settings finds its complement in accessories which display a touch of the exotic in mood or design.

Flowers and furnishings can be used in Contemporary homes in the same way that fashion employs an intricate piece of jewelry to sharpen the appeal of a basic costume.

Three anthurium spathes, with interesting tropical overtones, are in the spirit of the exotic furnishings that surround it. Arranged to follow a curving line, the design is reinforced with big philodendron foliage that repeats the glossy texture as well as the shape of the flowers.

Aztec motif on pottery container makes its contribution to the total composition, but is not so bold that it becomes a distracting influence.

←

Coordinate the color schemes of flowers and room furnishings

The ingredients of this arrangement—snaps, chrysanthemums, and croton leaves—are rich in appeal. But they do not account for the dramatic success of this design. Rather, it is the tapering shape and the precise color coordination between flowers and room setting that make it memorable. In addition, size of arrangement is correctly related to location

→

Use natural contrasts of foliage for fresh-looking Modern designs

Sansevieria leaves touched with white, lacy branches of lycopodium to soften contrasts, and glossy cherry laurel foliage placed low make a richly varied foliage arrangement for a Modern interior. Black ceramic accessories showing the Scandinavian influence in their design are well placed to balance the branch of laurel flowing out in the opposite direction

Modern seeks bold and daring effects

A flair for the exotic motivates many of the gifted arrangers who specialize in contemporary styles of flower arrangement.

There are no restrictions or limitations on types of containers, or on combinations of materials and colors—other than one's own artistic judgment of what is harmonious and fitting. The goal is to make original use of striking colors, forms, textures.

Jack Fredric Daniels, who created all of these arrangements, is an outstanding designer and teacher of the Modern school of arranging. His classes, at the College of San Mateo, California, are enthusiastically attended by professionals and amateurs.

Interest in both line and design are evident in this arresting flower and foliage composition. Ti leaves—a Hawaiian import—shape a triangular frame for 11 peony-carnations. Stems are inserted on a holder with a watercup so no water shows on flat plate

Modern puts ceramic birds in a nature scene

Instead of placing ceramic figures at one side of a composition—as accessories—Modern arrangements frequently include them as an essential part of the whole. Stylized nature scene shown here is an illustration of this type of design.

Two ceramic birds are the center of interest. Framing them are three natural tree fungi and a curved row of echeveria (hen-and-chickens) in graduated sizes. Polished burl base unifies this waterless arrangement.

←

Span the seasons in a blend of fresh and dried materials

As a break with Traditional reluctance to combine fresh and dried materials, Modern tries for a provocative blending of the seasons by inserting five mums in an otherwise all-dried materials arrangement.

Palm spathe, contorted palm leaf, and two branches of dried salal foliage frame the living blooms.

Pillow vase on a teakwood base is first filled with coarse gravel and water. Moisture will not harm the dried materials and keeps the chrysanthemums turgid and fresh.

→

Line-mass arrangement in an exact two-color scheme

Modern arrangers do not rule out multicolor schemes. But they frequently experiment with achieving satisfying variation in a composition while using only a limited color palette—such as the orange and green scheme shown here.

Strelitzia (bird-of-paradise) flowers, and croton leaves include both orange and green. Rubber-plant foliage is solid green. Surprise inclusions are the vivid lobster shells.

Artful simplicity can be the goal

At the opposite end of a Modern arranger's fascination with the exotic—illustrated by the arrangements shown on preceding pages—is his concern with the art of simplicity. It leads him to use foliage, seed pods, even weeds, in ways which Traditional arrangers would customarily reject.

But perhaps the seemingly opposite concerns are only two faces of a single coin: the desire to place one's signature on an arrangement so that it is unmistakably his.

Certainly it is exciting to demonstrate skill, taste, creative talent by using ingredients which others would scorn, and yet arrive at an artistically satisfying design.

Inspired by rustic simplicity

Anchor a piece of moss-covered driftwood—or use a gnarled branch that you've seasoned on the ground—and let it soar upward from a low bowl container. Use chrysanthemums sparingly for color and contrast of fresh with dry material. Many varieties of dried seed heads make good fillers for arrangement

←

Color and shape make a satisfying composition

A complementary color scheme of nature's skilled blending, plus the attractive shape of the caladium leaf are the basic ingredients of this foliage design.

The added quality that makes it an interesting arrangement is a careful placement that lets each leaf stand alone, yet be part of the satisfying total composition.

→

Sharp contrasts between simple materials make this arrangement attractive. Soft texture of the button mums makes glossy sheen of the single castor-bean leaf much more apparent.

Spearlike glad leaves return to dull texture, but repeat the pointed form of castor-bean leaf edges. Design is by Carl Starker.

Imitating fall's dry nature

Dock seed panicles are used to advantage in an arrangement meant for wintertime enjoyment. Chunk of worm-eaten wood at right gives solidity at the base to balance the upward sweep of interestingly curled dried leaf forms. Shiny copper bowl is a foil for the dry, dull textures of the arrangement itself

Changing seasons supply a theme

Autumn—with hints of winter to come—is captured in this arrangement. The bare stump of osage-orange says winter is close at hand. But the fresh ferns and chrysanthemums springing up from its base say nature's not yet completely dormant, and remind us to enjoy the last of the growing season

Queen-Anne's-lace (wild carrot weed) whitens roadsides everywhere, but too few of us take advantage of the snowflake beauty of its flower heads in arrangements. Here, stems are placed in an ascending rhythm to make the most of natural charms, some heads faced forward, others up in arrangement by Carl Starker

Key them to their background
to get the most from your flowers

Full bouquet of tulips in an informal setting

Mass arrangement of vibrant red tulips splashed with yellow is right in both style and color for its casual and invitingly summery indoor-outdoor setting.

Informal wrought-iron furniture upholstered in cool blue-green flowered fabric calls for a vivid color contrast and an unstudied bouquet of flowers.

It's easy to see that a strictly formal arrangement of pale, pastel flowers would not suit.

The heavy, stoneware container is also well chosen for harmony with the setting. It's in the same garden mood as the furniture, with a sturdy base that keeps this large and spreading arrangement from looking top-heavy.

←

Oriental arrangement in tune with Modern room

A room setting which typifies a Modern trend toward keeping large surfaces plain, shows its interest in detail with accessories.

In keeping with sophistication of wall plaque, lamp base, piece of sculpture is the Moribana arrangement of ti leaves and carnations. The container, burl base, and large black rock disguising the holder all add to the finished look. Arranged by Minoru Saito, Flower Master.

→

Style and color to blend with Traditional

Bright hues and unpretentious air of a marigold bouquet make it a nice accent for a living room furnished in a Traditional but informal manner. Test rightness of the arrangement by imagining instead an exotic, Modern design; obviously, flowers and room would suffer

Use flowers as decorating accents

"Use flowers for accents," is the advice of decorators. And we all realize how much the right arrangement can do for any room.

Flowers are lovely in themselves, but if we want to use them as decorating accents, it's important to consider the color, style, and size of an arrangement in relation to the room where it's to be placed.

Color—dealt with at greater length in the section which follows—is a relatively easy choice if room schemes are predominantly warm or cool. Opposites—cool with warm, and vice versa—do most for each other. In a neutral scheme, use vivid flower colors.

Choose an appropriate style

As important as color is the style of the flowers you use as decorative assets. Modern and Oriental arrangements are "naturals" for Contemporary rooms. Elaborate, Traditional bouquets look best in similar surroundings. And whatever the style, suit size of arrangement to size of place for display.

*Neutral color scheme
in a Contemporary room
invites a warm accent*

Contemporary furniture and fabrics which run largely to sandy beiges and browns welcome a spicy, warm touch which is provided by a modern arrangement of amaryllis blooms, bronzy mums, and colorful croton foliage.

Pyramid shape of the arrangement and its symmetrical design were good choices for a bouquet placed in a location where it can be seen from all sides.

Size of the arrangement is in scale with the amount of space devoted to its display—neither too large nor too small.

Container has simplicity of line which suits the chaste air of the room's furnishings. Its dark color is in good contrast to the light shades that predominate elsewhere in the room.

This flower arrangement was designed by Mrs. Tommy Bright.

Green and white have a fresh and cool look against warm wood tones

The increasing use of wood surfaces and wood paneling in today's homes accounts partially for the growing popularity of all-foliage or mostly foliage arrangements, with some flowers added, as in the one pictured.

Reasons for this are twofold: foliage green makes a beautiful contrast for the warm, reddish tones of many woods. Secondly, a foliage arrangement maintains the same informality that characterizes many rooms in which wood paneling is used: the family room, study, or den.

Here, camellia branch, white snaps, white peonies plus some yellow chrysanthemums provide fresh contrasts with wood tones.

Advance an Oriental theme in decorating with branches of bamboo

An Oriental influence is apparent in many home furnishings of taste and distinction—as in the gleaming metal hardware used on the ebony chest, and the grass cloth applied to the far wall of this modern living room.

Tall branches of bamboo, which need little arranging, have an exotic appeal that makes them appropriate in rooms displaying an Oriental influence.

Although it's on the expensive side to order through your florist, it does stay fresh many months, and even continues to put out fresh green leaves indoors.

Settings influence the size, color, and shape of arrangements

Tawny hues and simple styling are suited to a Provincial dining room

Low, symmetrically shaped centerpiece uses colors related to wood tones of a Provincial-style dining room. Croton leaves and foliage in arrangement supply green contrast to yellow and bronze hues that predominate. Simplicity of table flowers is also indicated by the informal pottery dishes and simple place mats with which the table is set

Good design counts if space for your flower arrangements is limited

Small rooms respond to the decorator touch of flowers quite as much as large ones do. But it can be difficult to know how to place them attractively without overcrowding.

Here's one way to solve the problem: suit style and design of flower arrangement to available space.

Two roses, with some of their foliage, are nestled into a spray of three pine branches in low container on an occasional table. Curve of the greenery takes into account the shape of the lampshade and gives a pleasing sense of balance.

If you have a dozen roses, and no one space large enough to display all 12, split them up into several smaller groups—with one of them like this.

Use generous proportions for an arrangement to fill a big wall space

Here's the reverse of the problem we dealt with above: a large, free wall space demands flower arrangements of generous proportions. Try to imagine the small arrangement pictured above substituted for the soaring foliage and glad arrangement which was used. You'll see for yourself what a difference appropriate scale makes to effect

Bring flowers into decorating schemes by applying color harmony

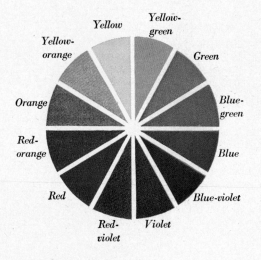

Skillful use of color improves any flower arrangement and makes it easy to get just the effect you want

←

Colors shown on this wheel are the simplest or "purest" ones. They have been neither shaded nor tinted. If you add white to one of these basic hues, you get pastel *tints* such as many flowers display. Added black produces *shades* or grayed colors most often used in decorating

There's nothing hard to learn about color harmony when it's applied to flowers. Nature's own color blends are so deft that it takes small skill to use them effectively.

Unlike pigments made by man, nature's colors are never "pure." Reds shade off to purple, and oranges to yellow in a single flower, so we shouldn't attempt to match flower colors to decorating schemes as we match paints.

Learning from the color wheel

Even though flowers are not exact reproductions of hues on a color wheel, we can learn a great deal from it about combining flower colors and using them to decorate.

The *monochromatic* color scheme is the simplest of color harmonies to recognize. It is merely a combination of the weaker and the stronger intensities of a single hue. Pink, rose, and red, used together, are a familiar example of monochromatic color harmony.

Next, look for the *primary* colors. They are red, yellow, and blue. Various blends of the three account for all other hues on the wheel. Yellow and red we call "warm" colors; blue is "cool." Notice that warm colors are concentrated on left side of wheel; cool on the right. Combine a warm and a cool color to achieve a pleasing effect.

Now pick out the opposite or *complementary* colors. They're the pairs which are exactly opposite each other on the wheel: violet is the complement of yellow; red of green. You get best effects from flower arrangements in complementary color harmony if they have a neutral background.

Analogous or neighboring colors are those next to each other on color wheel. Each contains much of its neighbor's hue, and they frequently make good partners.

Relate flowers to room colors

If you like to make decorative assets of flower arrangements, you'll want to consider flower color schemes in relation to the color schemes of rooms where they're placed.

On the following pages we show rooms decorated in monochromatic, complementary and analogous color schemes, with practical and easy-to-follow suggestions on ways to choose flowers for your home.

Try warm with cool

Yellow—a warm color—is a good choice for flowers to dress up a cool, blue room. Pink and red flowers in the picture are effective for same reason—their warmth

How about white?

White is a combination of all colors, so it's always safe to use a white flower in any room—no matter what its color scheme. But white won't lend warmth to a room

Violets are good

The violet hues will almost all be right in a blue room because they're "neighbors" of blue on the color wheel and have much blue in them, with a bit of red for warmth

This room, decorated in a monochromatic color scheme, with various tints and shades of blue, has an appealing, cool look. But it would look *cold* if there were no dashes of warm color—supplied here largely with flowers. If the room were decorated in a warm monochromatic scheme of reds or yellows, you'd want an opposite—cooling—effect from the flowers used in it

More ways to use flowers for color effects

Aim at a medley rather than a riot of color

when you want flowers to add beauty to your home,

and harmonize with your scheme of decoration

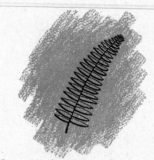

Green's always good

Take a lesson from nature, and feel free to put green in the picture, no matter what the color scheme. It's coupled with flowers of every hue—and always looks right

An analogous room scheme uses two neighbors of the blue which predominates: green and violet. Then it adds a touch of yellow in the gold lamp shades. For a room scheme as intricate as this, your best cue is to use tints or shades of one of the colors already present—or white. Reds introduced should be on the violet side. Adding more "pure" hues would produce a garish effect

May we use blue?

Blue flowers would not be *wrong* in either of the two rooms pictured. But they'd only add more blue to one room, and be lost in a red-green scheme in the other

What will a red do?

Tints of shades of red will work in either of these two rooms. For the blue-purple scheme, pick reds that lean toward violet. Clear red is a better choice in the other

Use restraint in choosing flowers for a complementary color scheme room

In rooms decorated with definite complementary color harmonies (here, red-green), best choice of flower colors is usually among the tints and shades of two colors already used. In addition, green and white will always be good. Small amount of yellow in arrangement pictured harmonizes with gold tones of the wood-paneled walls and is also quite acceptable

Pick a number from one to twelve

Next time you buy—or are given—a dozen of one kind of flower, play the game of dividing the florists' dozen into two or three arrangements. It's more fun than using all of them in one bouquet, and it pays big dividends of fresh beauty for several locations in your home—not just one.

New tricks with twelve

First, decide on the places where you want to put the groups of flowers. Will it be in the center of the dining table, on the buffet, on a hall, occasional, or coffee table? Perhaps a desk needs brightening.

Next, choose containers to suit the locations you've chosen to decorate with flowers. Use tall vases or low bowls, depending upon the amount of height that you are seeking.

Now divide the bunch into the groupings you've decided on. If one of the arrangements is to consist of a single flower—as in the one across the page—choose the biggest, most perfect bloom for it. Attention will focus on it—just because it's alone—more sharply than on individual blooms in arrangements that include several.

Play up the foliage, too

Florists ordinarily include extra foliage—salal, huckleberry, or other greens with a bunch. Often the blooms have their own luxurious foliage, like the leaves on the roses we've used for our demonstration. Let the foliage help you to fill in and vary designs.

The perfection of one rose has universal appeal

Here's a way to use a single rose so it's an "arrangement" in itself.

This design uses salal (commonly called lemon leaves) to make a green frame for a glowing, single rose.

If your roses—or other flowers—have good, fresh foliage, you can use it equally as effectively to expand the dimensions and important look of one bloom in similar fashion.

This container—an appealing ceramic imitation of a seashell—contributes its share to the dramatic appearance of the flower in both shape and sharp color contrast.

Combine the beauty of crystal and roses in a simply styled arrangement using two blooms

Handsome crystal goblet makes an imaginative substitute for a conventional vase, although a bud vase would be equally suitable for two-flower arrangements like this one.

The two roses, with their own foliage, were cut to different lengths and inserted in tiny needlepoint holder which was first secured in bottom of goblet with florists' clay. Additional foliage was inserted for attractive fullness.

After the roses and foliage had been placed, some clear-glass marbles were dropped in to disguise stem patterns and add further interest.

If you want a low centerpiece for your dining-room table, here's a way to use the other nine roses

Rose stems are held in place by piece of hardware cloth that covers top of vase. It's out of sight, thanks to careful foliage placement.

Roses were cut to varying stem lengths and faced in slightly different directions so each diner would have an equally attractive view of the arrangement. Notice that largest blooms are placed lowest—one on this side, the other in corresponding opposite position, on the side of vase which is away from you in the picture.

This arrangement and the two others on this page were designed by Mrs. Cummins Rawson.

A quartet of quick arrangements

*Try these easy-to-do arrangements
if you're a beginner—or whenever you
have a few flowers and limited time*

Never feel that you must have an arm-
load of gorgeous blooms and hours of time
before you can attempt an arrangement.

It's fun to splurge when flowers and time
are unlimited. But it's equally as rewarding to show what you can do with a few
flowers in a short space of time. In flower
arranging, as in any art, it's what you do
with what you have that counts.

The true joy of flower arranging lies in
active rather than passive participation.
It is more gratifying to design a simple
flower arrangement yourself than to admire someone else's superb creation.

We show you four easy-to-do arrangements. None uses more than seven flower
stems and a small amount of foliage. All
can be duplicated in less than a half-hour.

←

Seven stems of yellow narcissus and just a little
self-foliage are all it takes for this arrangement.
A small needlepoint holder in the bottom of
the Japanese Usubata container—or any low
bowl would do—holds the stems in place. Inspired by the Oriental style, it uses three stems to
establish a triangle; the others fill in the design

→

Pink gerberas with their own foliage in a green bottle
(it's a commercial prune juice bottle) show their slanting stems interestingly through the clear glass of the
container. The small, black base helps balance height of
foliage, gives a more finished look to a simple arrangement. Many common garden flowers would lend themselves well to similar designs, take only a matter of minutes to arrange. Arrangement designed by Carl Starker

Display graceful lines of blooms, stems, and foliage by arranging Japanese iris in a shallow bowl

When you buy Japanese iris from your florist, see if you can find one still in bud to use as the tallest stem in a simple line arrangement similar to this one.

Slant the remaining flower stems slightly to right and left of tallest stalk, each stem shorter than the one that preceded it. You want every flower head to remain separate from the others. Cut the last flower stem very short and face bloom forward.

When all of the stalks are in place, add small amounts of the foliage to fill in the design. Don't permit stem lines to cross one another as you make your additions.

This arrangement includes seven Japanese iris, but you could use five or nine with approximately the same effect. Garden iris make good substitutes when in season.

Needlepoint holder in which stems are secured is disguised with small white rocks.

This gladiolus arrangement takes just seven blooming stalks and a few spears of fresh foliage

An arrangement of seven gladiolus stalks is indebted for its design to the Japanese Moribana style, though it does not adhere strictly to the placement or proportions of that school of Oriental arranging.

It depends for effect on using flowering stalks of varying lengths, some facing forward, others toward the main stem in group. Shorter stalks were placed in foreground to disguise bare stems of tallest ones and to help concentrate the viewer's attention on one central portion in the arrangement.

A few spears of glad foliage were inserted after all blooms had been placed. Their function is to fill in bare spots between stems and give a flowing look to the whole.

The shallow round container is a Japanese bronze flower bowl. Its dark color and that of the rock which disguises the needlepoint holder were chosen to lend satisfying contrast to the pale tints of gladiolus blooms.

This arrangement and those of iris and narcissus were designed by Mrs. Theodore Stroud.

Arrange these
in just
three minutes

A single glad spike with a ruff of philodendron leaves is displayed in an Eighteenth Century porcelain basket which holds a cup for water. All of the undeveloped buds were first removed from end to get color right up to the tip of the flower spike. Both glad spike and the philodendron leaves are secured on a needlepoint holder

Colorful hibiscus blooms are pretty in a pitcher or floating in a saucer

If you have beautiful flowering shrubs in your garden, do clip a few of the blooms and branches— judiciously, of course, so as not to injure the plant—to put on display inside your house; you can enjoy their perfection more fully when they are at close range.

There needn't be anything fussy about the arrangement. Select an informal type of container to contrast in color, texture with the plant material. Prune as necessary to emphasize free-flowing, natural growth lines.

A flower floating in a saucer of water makes a cool-looking room-freshener for almost any spot in a house when summer heat comes.

A single canna and its own foliage give you quick color

If you have never thought of using cannas in a flower arrangement, here is evidence that you've been missing a good summertime bet.

Get an easy splash of color with 1 canna spike cut to 1½ or 2 times the diameter of a shallow container. Center on a small needlepoint holder.

Cut 6 leaves and arrange to encircle blooming stalk as pictured. Place two of the larger leaves low as shown, giving breadth at the base of your single-flower composition.

Place small pebbles to disguise the needlepoint holder.

Composition in yellow and red

Bright red ash tray serves as container for one Chinese peony and a few deeply notched leaves. Place the leaves on a needlepoint holder first so they'll be high enough to protect peony flower petals from water soaking

Vine tendrils have graceful curves

Three tendrils of morning-glory vine with one flower fully open and several tight buds are graceful in a ceramic bud vase. Let one vine end come forward and rest on the table. Other annual vines that might be arranged very similarly are: sweetpeas, trailing nasturtium, moonflower, hyacinth bean, and gourds

Make a virtue of simplicity with easy arrangements that anyone can do

Most of us would like nothing better than to have flowers always about the house. We know that they add freshness and beauty in a way that nothing else can do.

But we often forego that pleasure because we haven't fully realized the possibilities of simplicity, and the attractive results we might get with just a few flowers.

Simplicity *does* have real charm, and it is basic to the design of all the arrangements pictured on these two pages. Three of them include only two stalks of bloom plus foliage. The other two contain more flowers, but they are easy to arrange, and completely casual in their effect.

Don't do without flowers when it's so easy —and inexpensive—to have them about.

Two lovely roses in a white ceramic bud vase are the simple ingredients of this arrangement. Curving line of stem, glossiness of foliage, freshness of bloom make you want to look, and look again. Use roses from your garden—or from florist—to duplicate this arrangement at any time of the year

Take maximum advantage of the magnificence of flag iris in a two-bloom arrangement. Cut stalks that include buds as well as open flowers; include some spears of iris foliage to get contrast of pointed leaf shape with the round form of flowers. Japanese iris wi'l look well in similar arrangements

Generous use of foliage makes just two stalks of daylilies seem important. A frosty glass bottle container gives a refreshingly cool look to the arrangement. Cut stalks that include buds as well as open blooms, for daylilies do live up to the name — last just a day

Short-stemmed double tulips, of several different colors, are inserted on a needlepoint holder and displayed in a shallow leaf-shaped bowl. For best effect, keep the yellows high, reds low

Arrange garden iris the easy way
and show off each bloom's perfection

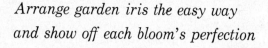

1 Cut tallest stalk 1½ times length of bowl. Place at center back of the holder. Add second iris ⅔ height of tallest; slant to right. Third stem is ½ the height of first. Place low, slanting to left, as pictured

2 Add four more stalks of yellow iris; every stem should be a different length. Insert two stalks to the right and two to the left of central stalk. Use some iris foliage to accent flowing lines of the design

3 Fill central pocket with four bronzy-purple (any dark shade will do) iris. Each stalk should be of a different length from all the others. Cut last stem shortest of all and insert at center front. Face bloom directly forward

Chapter 2

These make flower arranging easy

Like any art or craft, flower arranging requires good equipment. But the essentials are relatively few and inexpensive.

All you really need—other than flowers—are: three or four containers in the basic shapes; an assortment of needlepoint and wire flower holders; a sharp knife or flower shears, some florists' tape and clay.

Consider containers first

Shape, size, and color of containers are of first importance. Until you become a collector of bowls and vases, shun the ones that are bright in color, strikingly patterned.

Neutral shades of off-white, green, gray, beige, and brown won't compete with flower hues. For the infrequent occasions when you *do* want a vivid container, see if you can't make use of things you have about the house.

You'll be adequately equipped for making both large and small arrangements if you remember the importance of good proportion between size of bouquet and container and choose a variety of containers accordingly.

Mechanical aids are important

Needlepoint and wire holders are the foundation of flower arrangements. They must be big and heavy enough to establish balance.

You'll want an assortment of sizes and shapes, but all holders should be heavy and rustproof. Strong, sharp points are essential for the needlepoint type of holder.

A sharp knife is a possible substitute for flower shears, but it's more dangerous, less satisfactory for woody stems and branches.

Florists' tape and clay

Waterproof clay will anchor needlepoint holder firmly when you're arranging tall, heavy stems that might topple. One valuable use for florists' tape is to add thickness to stems too thin to be secured in needlepoint.

A relaxed attitude helps you get the most pleasure possible when you're arranging flowers

Nothing is more relaxing than flower arranging if you approach it properly. Select and gather together the equipment you'll need. Spread it out on a table. Be seated and prepare to enjoy the process in an unhurried mood.

Of course there are times when you must hurry. But don't expect arrangements done under pressure to be your best, or to bring the most pleasure.

If you seek an outlet for creative self-expression, you'll be rewarded by each hour you spend in arranging flowers.

Good tools are your best helpers

Needlepoint and wire flower holders in assorted sizes and shapes are *musts*. So are really sharp flower shears or knife. Florists' clay and tape are useful aids. Rubber bottle with spray cap lets you send a mist of water over a completed arrangement keeping it fresh and crisp for a longer period

Basic shapes for flower bowls and vases

If you're starting a collection of flower containers, begin with four similar to these basic shapes: low, round bowl; shallow, rectangular one; tall, columnar vase; tall, rectangular or pillow vase. An average size for such containers would be from 9 to 12 inches in height or width

Equipment for the "flower master"

A fine collection of equipment marks the truly expert flower arranger—even though he does not hold the charming title "Flower Master" which Oriental schools of arranging confer on talented graduates.

The beginner need not—in fact, should not—rush out to buy everything he sees on the market. But as skill and taste increase, so does the desire for additional tools to help give arrangements a finished look.

Shown here are samples of the multitude of aids to flower arranging that are on the market. As your enthusiasm and your ability grow, you'll want to add more and more of them to your own group of favorites.

Store it all in one spot

Whether your collection of flower arranging equipment is large or small, you'll enjoy using it more if it's conveniently stored.

A handy shelf is fine for a beginner. The advanced arranger needs more space—such as the storage unit pictured across the page, with drawers and shelves to keep everything in place—ready for use when it's wanted.

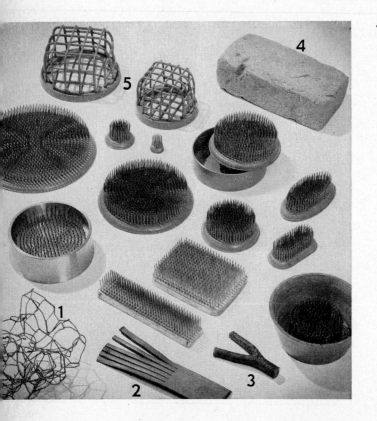

◄ Needlepoint holders will probably be your favorite, but there are times when you'll want to use other types of holders.

Crumpled chicken wire (1) is good for stuffing opaque vases. For glass vases, use a strip of plumber's lead (2); wrap it around neck of bouquet, hooking an end over lip of vase. Use foliage to hide it. Forked sticks (3) are also useful to hold stems in place in tall vases.

Nonspillable water (4) and cupholders are good when a container's too shallow to hold water. Use wire cage-holders (5) to secure long, thick stems of flowers and foliage in Traditional arrangements.

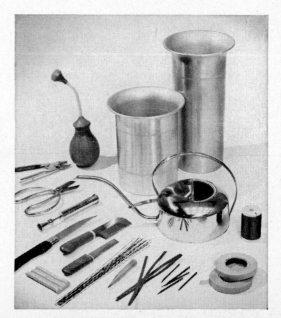

Keep these tools and aids handy to make ➡ flower arranging easier. Wilting blooms, weak stems, unsteady needlepoint holders are easily corrected if your kit includes a sharp clippers, scissors, a water spray, florists' wire, clay, tape, picks, and thread. Have several tall cans (you can use commercial cans with tops removed) on hand to hold flowers while they're conditioning

An especially designed storage unit has easy-to-get-at drawers and shelves that will accommodate an extensive collection of flower arranging equipment.

Largest sections are flexible because of slots that let you move shelves or partitions around to make room for the unusually shaped items you may want to keep in the storage cabinet.

Shallow drawers at the top of the unit are convenient for storing all the small items, such as needlepoint and wire holders, clay, tape, wire, shears, and so on. Pull-out cutting board is convenient.

Whether or not you're an enthusiast for ➤ the Oriental style of flower arranging, you'd enjoy using a Japanese arranger's kit. The one shown includes heavy blades for woody branches; tiny saw for pruning; shears and a syringe for mist-spraying. Rocks and pebbles, forked sticks, needlepoint holders, florists' tape and fine wire complete the set of accessories, equipment

Tricks of the trade that help to make

How to prune branches of foliage and camouflage those necessary cuts

◄ Woody branches frequently need some pruning and shaping for beauty of line. But leaving exposed cuts visible spoils the appearance of an arrangement — makes it look amateurish. Always make a clean, slanting cut *directly behind base* of stem that's to show. Now take piece of branch you clipped off and rub it over cut surface. Enough bark "dye" will come off to darken cut, make it quite inconspicuous

Use florists' tape if you need to lengthen a too-short flower stem

If a stem is too short for proper placement of a ► bloom, you can make it longer by adding an extra piece of stem clipped off elsewhere; use florists' tape to bind the two together as shown. Be sure to leave the original stem end free to absorb water and long enough so that it does reach the water

Forked stick serves to hold stems in place in a deep container

◄ For deeper flower containers, use a fitted, forked stick to hold flower stems in place. They are especially good for any container that has a wide mouth but is too deep for convenient use of needle-point holders to secure the stems. To make, cut V into a single stick and bind with wire to prevent further splitting. Or use one that is naturally forked. Buy ready-made ones imported from Japan

flower arrangements look professional

An ordinary toothpick can be used to repair a drooping flower head

◆ Drooping heads of all hollow-stemmed flowers, such as zinnias and chrysanthemums, can be repaired with an ordinary toothpick. Plunge the sharply pointed tip straight through the middle of the bloom and down into stem as far as possible. Be careful not to let the toothpick pierce through stem covering. Keep a supply of these toothpicks with your equipment so they'll be handy as such emergencies arise

Disguise a shiny needlepoint holder with green florists' tape

When you are doing a flower arrangement in a low ➤ container, it's important to camouflage the needlepoint holder. If it's shiny—or paint's chipped—wrap it with green florists' tape. Start at the top and work downward diagonally, pulling and stretching tape as you work so it will have a smooth finish

Florists' clay will anchor your needlepoint holder securely in a bowl

◆ Tall arrangements in shallow containers will be in no danger of toppling over if you will anchor the needlepoint holder with waterproof florists' clay. Take a piece of clay and roll it between palms of your hands to get length you need. Have container absolutely dry. Place thin roll of clay in circle of same size as needlepoint. Press holder down on clay and it will not loosen when the water's added

It's satisfying to own the right containers

Metal containers in Oriental style

These bronze containers are especially well suited to Oriental-style arrangements. Low bowl is good for Moribana groupings; taller vases (one in right foreground is actually a tea gong with mallet) are best for informal Nageire or "throw-in" style of arrangements

The simplicity of white pottery

Chaste white and off-white containers are worthwhile items for anyone's collection of basic flower bowls and vases. Very similar shapes are available in other neutral hues, but white is often just the contrast you'll want to make vivid flower colors sing. Word of caution: don't use these on the table unless they relate well to your china pattern

Choose colored glass as a flattering companion to many kinds of flowers

Carnations—or any flowers with petals of fine, silky texture—are perfect in glass containers. And when glass is tinted, you get nice color contrast, too.

Look about you. Chances are you possess a number of glass bowls, pitchers, bottles, or vases similar to those pictured. Or you can buy them inexpensively.

Maybe they weren't originally intended to hold flowers, but if they add variety and style to unpretentious arrangements, by all means use them whenever suitable.

Glazed ceramic bowls are inexpensive

You'll find many good-looking and inexpensive pottery containers on the market. Use a big one, like scalloped bowl at top, to emphasize the shape of a round dining table. Small ring at left is perfect for short-stemmed flowers like pansies or violets. Rectangular bowl's good for either fruit or flowers

Containers in the modern manner

The contemporary look of these ceramic containers makes them appropriate for the most modern of arrangements. Unusual textures, patterns, shapes require that you exercise care lest they outbid flower arrangements for interest. Make use of strong lines and bold flower colors you are certain will compete successfully

Modern reproductions of antique holders suit traditional bouquets

Here's a sampling of the many faithful reproductions on today's market of antique objects especially suited to traditional nosegays or bouquets. In the group pictured are a pitcher of classic lines, an English hunting horn of mahogany (metal lined to hold water), a milkglass urn, and a glass-bottomed pewter mug

Select flower containers that will blend with their surroundings

When you buy flower containers, ask yourself whether they'll blend with the style of furnishings in your home. Those pictured here are Modern in design, but unobtrusive enough to suit almost any setting. The three shallow containers have the added advantage of being able to double as serving dishes if you like

Use nature's art in your arrangements

Set springtime yellow against soft green of a lichen-covered rock

Miniature scenes from nature take their inspiration from those Japanese arrangements which attempt to capture the spirit rather than the actuality of a landscape.

Notice how the subtle green of a lichen-covered rock makes yellow primroses and forsythia seem even more springlike and inviting.

Take time when you go for a walk in the woods to seek out interesting pieces of wood and rock that you can use in compositions like this.

Shells have their own fascination

All the pleasures of seashore strolls, gathering shells as you go, are recalled by an arrangement such as this. With the seashells are slender grasses, azalea foliage and shoots of strawberry groundcover. The composition is displayed in three shallow glass plates of various sizes

Weathered wood can be decorative

The bold simplicity of a large chunk of wood and its interesting texture are the dominant feature of this arrangement. Delicate ferns, grasses, and foliage emphasize the solidity of the wood by contrast. The rocks in the foreground disguise mechanics of the arrangement

Pieces of wood that look like sculpture are yours for the finding

Here are samples of nature's sculpture which you may have for nothing more than the trouble of searching them out in your travels: a manzanita branch, a water-smoothed fragment of driftwood, and a twisted piece of sagebrush. Each one you find will be different from any other, and used in your arrangements will give them a unique quality. Hunt for wood of interesting shape, texture, color for your collection

Gather shells for beauty of form

The infinite variety—and appeal—of shells is too seldom taken advantage of by flower arrangers. Look to them as a rich source of intricate patterns, shapes, and colors. Use them imaginatively in your arrangements of plant materials that normally grow near the water

Don't forget rocks and pebbles

It pays to be a "rock hound" when flower arranging's your hobby. Of course you use rocks and pebbles to disguise needlepoint holders. But don't forget that they can be extremely effective as the dominant feature in an arrangement that seeks to imitate a landscape

When to use figurines with flowers

When to use figurines is always a question. The best answer seems to be that they should be used if they help to tell the story or advance the theme of the flower arrangement you've created.

If they're just an afterthought, or if they have no real beauty of their own, they should be omitted as distractions rather than additions to the loveliness of the flowers themselves.

On these pages are some examples of artistic and tasteful ways to use figurines in or with flower compositions.

A graceful Madonna, surrounded by Easter lilies and yellow tulips sets a religious theme with taste and restraint.

Statuette was secured in center of holder with florists' clay. Then tulips, with some of their own foliage, were inserted as background to Madonna.

Short-stemmed Easter lilies, each a different length, face forward and up.

Oriental springtime scene

Japanese goddess of mercy stands in a bower of flowering cherry branches, on a bed of white pebbles. Cupholder behind the figurine supplies water and secures branches. Arrangement by Carl Starker

A gardener makes a subtle boast

An amusing green glass frog, his eyes incredulous at the sight, calls attention to the magnificence of some perfect blooms of tuberous begonia. Neutral straw mat emphasizes the brilliant color of both the begonia blooms and the glass frog

Figurines of beautiful design

When you buy figurines, it's worthwhile to invest in ones with real beauty of design. Several of those pictured here are imports from England, Denmark, and Austria. All are in good taste.

Oriental arrangers never place figurines in water unless they represent animals that normally live in or under the water. It's a good general rule for all flower arrangers to keep in mind.

Tranquil nature scene shows a duck resting in the shade of a tree at the water's edge, with grasses growing nearby. To represent tree are branches of nandina. Small foliage includes blue creeping campanula, Japanese anemones, and strawberry begonia. The arrangement was designed by Mabel Hoyt

Bases for flower arrangements

To give a finished look to a flower arrangement, many arrangers use a base. It may be of teak, straw, bamboo, polished wood of all sorts. Or it might even be a mirror, since they are now returning to vogue.

In addition to the sense of completeness which a base or mat can provide, it may do two other things: extend the dimensions of an arrangement so that it more adequately fills a large area; or improve the apparent balance of a tall flower composition in a slender, elongated vase.

When selecting a base, keep in mind the style of the arrangement—formal or informal—and chose one to match. Unless you're sure they're harmonious, omit the base.

1 To start, you need a tree stump that has been weathered by sun, wind, and rain for at least several months. Osage orange—like this piece— is good choice because of hard, attractive grain. You could use oak, hard maple, cherry, or other fruit woods instead. Use a handsaw to remove an oblique slice from the stump to any thickness desired. Slightly more than a half-inch is usual

Instead of a bowl, use a burl base to display fall garden arrangements

Rich, brown wood tones of highly polished burl base blend with autumnal colors of fruits and vegetables in an arrangement to decorate an informal fall table.

Sprouted onion, well-scrubbed carrots are amusing additions to an edible centerpiece; they are unpretentious, however, and so should be included only if the occasion is a very casual one.

Burl bases themselves are not limited to use with strictly informal arrangements. They are in excellent taste as finishes for semiformal arrangements of Oriental or Modern style. Part of their appeal is their flexibility.

Ready-made burls come in many sizes and finishes. But if you're deft at simple carpentry, you can make your own by following instructions given above.

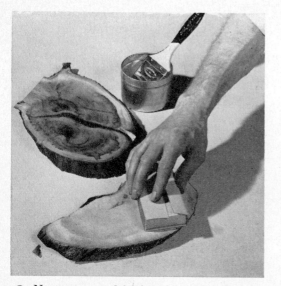

2 Next step: sand burl to a perfectly smooth surface. Wrap sandpaper around block of wood for easy handling. Use it to sand both sides until all roughness is gone. If wood color is too light to suit you, stain to desired shade. Next, brush with clear varnish. Let dry. Sand it again before applying the next coat of varnish—the more coats of varnish, the glossier your finish

3 Finished burls in assorted sizes have a number of uses in addition to serving as bases for your flower arrangements. They add to the effectiveness of a favorite statuette, or may be used as stands to protect table tops. One advantage of making your own burl bases is that you can have one the right size for each container. Be sure base is comfortably larger than the container

Choose a base to suit your arrangement

Ready-made stands for flower arrangements are on the market in all sizes, shapes, finishes. Samples pictured here include (reading clockwise from top): rectangular wood base on legs; similar base in light finish and more nearly square in shape; bamboo rods joined with cord to form a mat; a distinctive burl; two teakwood bases—larger one with scroll finish in lieu of feet. Choose from these and many more

Coarsely woven straw-cloth place mat makes an attractive base for arrangement of yellow snapdragons and ranunculus in an old wooden mortar used as a container. Pestle placed nearby and round woven tray as background complete the informal composition. It was designed by Dorothy Gleason

How to keep cut flowers longer

How to keep the appealing, dewy-freshness of cut flowers is a problem that interests every flower arranger. Whether the blooms be unassuming daisies from your garden, or aristocratic, long-stemmed roses from your florist, they'll look beautiful longer if you treat them properly.

The first thing to remember is that flowers must have an immediate and continuing supply of water, once they're cut, to replace the life-giving foods and fluids of the plant on which they grew. This water must be clean and fresh, *never cold, sometimes warm!*

When you cut garden flowers

Carry along a pail of water when you go into the garden. Have it about 110 degrees (quite warm). *You* may like ice water on a warm day, but your flowers don't. It shocks them; they can't drink it in as well as tepid water. Be sure, too, that flower shears or knife are very sharp. Dull instruments crush stems and make it impossible for them to absorb an adequate supply of water.

Flowers from your florist

About the same rules apply to prolonging the life of flowers from your florist as to the ones from your garden. They, too, need an immediate drink of water. Cut off tips of stems at an angle, with sharp knife or shears. "Condition" by placing in deep water for an hour or two before using in an arrangement.

Use any commercial flower foods or preservatives your florist may send with a bouquet. Or buy some to keep on hand. These blend the right amount of sugar and acidifier, strengthen flowers, reduce bacterial growth.

Cleanliness can reduce wilt

Use immaculately clean containers at every step—from the pail or deep pitcher you use for conditioning to the vase or bowl in which you arrange your flowers. Scrub containers with hot, soapy water after each use to eliminate the decay germs that hasten wilt. After the soap bath, rinse very thoroughly, for traces of soap left on containers will damage the flowers as much as the bacteria would.

Don't forget to include your needlepoint holder in the clean-up operations. It's a good idea to scald it occasionally with boiling hot water, since it's difficult to get between the needles with ordinary methods of cleaning.

Water temperature is important

When you "condition" newly cut flowers by giving them a deep drink before arranging, never use water that is below room or air temperature. Professionals let newly cut flowers stand for an hour or two in buckets of warm water. Then they move buckets and flowers into damp, refrigerated rooms. Garden flowers treated as nearly the same way as possible will "harden" better and be easier to work with, as well as longer lasting in your arrangements. When you are adding water to an arrangement to replace what has evaporated, be sure to use tepid water, not ice water, or water as cold as it runs from the tap

Special ways to treat stems

Stems of flowers or foliage may be scraped at the base with a sharp knife to permit greater water intake. When stems are thick, they may also be split upward from base for an inch or so. But be sure the scraped or split ends are completely submerged in water in finished arrangement. One of the virtues of the needlepoint holder is that its sharp points pierce stems as they are placed and help a good deal to ensure that water will be absorbed freely. Woody stems of foliage benefit from scraping, splitting, or even pounding. (See instructions for preparing lilac stems on page 77 which apply also to all woody branches)

Fresh-cut stems absorb more water

If a flower is out of water more than 5 to 10 minutes, always make a fresh base cut with a sharp knife or flower shears before reinserting in water. Stem tips exposed to the air will quickly form a sealing film which then keeps water from being absorbed in sufficient quantity to maintain freshness. Cut away all foliage which would be submerged in water in completed arrangement. Leaves under water decay quickly, look unattractive, and frequently have an unpleasant odor as well. Removing excess foliage is also important if you want beautiful, natural lines of flower and foliage stems to show in the completed design

Sear stems of certain flowers

There are a few flowers—most of which have a milky fluid in their stems—which wilt almost immediately unless you sear their stems promptly after cutting. Poinsettias are one example of this type of flower; you'll find others listed in the chart on the following page. To sear stem tips, use either a hot flame (a candle works well) or immerse tips of stems in boiling water for about 30 seconds. If you use this boiling water method, you must protect foliage and blooms from steam. One way is to thrust stem ends through sheets of tissue paper and gently hold the paper around them so that no steam gets to flowers

Avoid hot or drafty locations

If possible, put your bouquet where the temperature will be as even as possible—out of drafts, not near a radiator. But always place them where you'll enjoy them most; never let flowers waste away in a cool basement or refrigerator. Fill the container to its brim once your arrangement is completed. You needn't change water daily, but you should add it as needed to make up for evaporation losses. Keep bouquets fresh by removing and replacing the faded flowers and leaves. When a good many blooms have wilted but others are still fresh, do another arrangement on a smaller scale, and extend your pleasure

Tips on cutting and preparing flowers

Flower	When to cut and how to treat
Anemone	½ to fully open. Scrape stems
Aster	¾ to fully open. Scrape stems
Azalea	Bud to fully open. Scrape and crush stems
Bachelor-button	½ to fully open. Scrape stems
Bleedingheart	4 or 5 florets open. Scrape stems
Buddleia	¾ to fully open. Scrape stems or sear in flame
Calendula	Fully open. Scrape stems
Carnation	Fully open; snap or break from plant. Scrape stems
Canna	½ to fully open. Scrape stems
Chrysanthemum	Fully open. Break off and scrape stems or crush
Clematis	¾ to fully open. Scrape stems
Daffodil	As color shows in bud. Do not cut foliage or bulb will not mature. Scrape stems
Dahlia	Fully open. Sear stems in flame
Daisy	½ to fully open. Scrape stems or sear in flame
Daylily	¾ to fully open. Flowers last just one day
Delphinium	¾ to fully open. Scrape stems; snap off top buds
Geranium	Fully open. Scrape stems
Gerbera	¾ to fully open. Sear stems in flame
Gladiolus	As second floret opens. Scrape stems; snap off top buds
Grape-hyacinth	¾ to fully open. Scrape stems; do not cut foliage
Heliotrope	¾ to fully open. Sear stems in flame
Hollyhock	¾ to fully open. Float florets or scrape stems
Hydrangea	Fully open. Sear stems in flame
Iris	As first bud opens. Do not cut foliage; scrape stems
Larkspur	¾ to fully open. Scrape stems; snap off top buds
Lilac	½ to fully open. Scrape and crush stems; float wilted branches in 110-degree water for an hour
Marigold	Fully open. Scrape stems
Mignonette	¾ to fully open. Sear stems in flame
Morning-glory	In evening when closed. Wrap each bud in soft paper, sear vine stem; let stand in deep water overnight
Narcissus	As color shows. Do not cut foliage; scrape stems
Nasturtium	½ to fully open. Use with its own foliage
Peony	Bud in color to fully open. Scrape or split stems
Phlox	Fully open. Scrape stems
Poinsettia	Full color. Sear stems and points from which leaves have been removed
Poppy	Night before opening. Sear stems; drop of wax in heart of flower keeps it open
Rose	As second petal unfurls. Cut stem just above a five-petal leaf or plant will stop blooming. Scrape stems
Snapdragon	¾ to fully open. Scrape stems; snap off top buds
Stock	¾ to fully open. Scrape stems; snap off top buds
Sweetpea	¾ to fully open. Snap stem from vine
Tulip	Bud to ½ open. Do not cut foliage; scrape stems. Wrap flowers in paper; stand in deep water overnight
Violet	½ to fully open. "Harden" by soaking in water for half-hour then wrap and refrigerate
Waterlily	Tight bud. Sear stems in boiling water; drop of wax in heart of flower keeps it open
Zinnia	Fully open. Sear stems in flame

Chapter 3

Enjoy each of the seasons in its turn

A newly creative way of looking at every growing thing is one of the life-enriching pleasures that an interest in flower arranging brings with it.

> *"All seasons shall be sweet to thee*
> *Whether the summer clothe the general earth*
> *With greenness, or the redbreast sit and sing*
> *Betwixt the tufts of snow on the bare*
>   *branches*
> *Of mossy apple-tree."*
>   S. T. COLERIDGE

In the same way you savor the variations of the ever-changing seasons, try to express them in your arrangements. Spring, summer, autumn, winter—each has its individual pattern of growth. Yours be the challenge to symbolize a season with branch, bloom, leaf.

→

What's more springlike than a few branches of rosy, flowering crab in a bright blue bowl? Flowering branches, with vital, vigorous curves, call to mind the essence of the season—new growth appearing everywhere

Full, spreading arrangement of glads speaks eloquently of summer at its most perfect; includes buds, half and fully opened blooms on each stalk. Including all growth stages in your flower arrangement helps to symbolize the nature of midsummer

Summer, winter, autumn or spring—

each has its special virtues which

a flower arranger can symbolize with

bud and bloom, leaf and branch

Winter's the time—when most growing things are completely dormant—to test the imagination. Gnarled wood, some sprigs of evergreen, snow that looks almost real, tiny animals out searching for food, bespeak the season. A bit of winter brought into our comfortably warm homes makes the hearth more inviting

← Somewhat sparse branches, their leaves showing fall's rich coloring, say that summer's at an end for another year. We are reminded by the arrangement to enjoy to the full the flowers and the fruits of the harvest season while it lasts

Invite spring to come early

One day toward winter's end, when you feel you can't wait for spring to arrive, go cut some branches of flowering shrubs or trees for indoor forcing. Be judicious. You don't want to mutilate the parent plant, and you won't if you select branches that should be pruned later, anyway. You'll have best luck in forcing if you cut branches about a month before they'd be leafing out normally. Try to select those with lovely, natural curves so they'll make an interesting arrangement even when they're still bare. Give them lots of light, frequent doses of warm water; see buds swell and tiny leaves open.

Accommodating pussy willows

Easiest of all branches to force, pussy willows are also the most pliable and adaptable. Gently bend them into graceful curves and complement them with a splash of golden daffodils

Watch branches burst into beauty before spring arrives

Use branches of cherry, apple, peach, redbud, quince or spice bush to establish the main lines of an arrangement like this one. Choose shoots with lots of fat flower buds. Replace and rearrange an assortment of spring blooms at the base of the branches to keep your composition interesting.

For success in constructing an arrangement of flowering branches in a low container, it is absolutely essential to use a heavy, big needlepoint holder. Otherwise, branches will not stay in place; or completed arrangement may topple over and be ruined.

Follow our suggestions for preparing flowering branches on page 77 (tips on lilac stems apply to all flowering branches), and also on page 87. Be sure to hammer or split ends so branches can soak up ample supply of water. Spraying branches with water helps, too, but move arrangement to sink when you do this.

Bare branches and daffodils

Still-bare branches of flowering crab have a delicate tracery which needs only a handful of daffodils to bring spring indoors on the dreariest of late-winter days. See how leaves, then flowers open out in the two pictures we show just below

Daisies replace the daffodils

Now the little green leaves have begun to appear on the flowering crab branches. This will happen in about one week's time in the warmth of your home. Try some yellow daisies as new focal point for this arrangement

Branches burst into bloom

During the third and fourth weeks after you bring the branches of flowering crab indoors, the delicate pink flowers should appear. Add an assortment of blooms to keep arrangement fresh and sunshiny as a spring day

Use spring's bounty of flowering bulbs and branches that go so well together

Spring's budding branches and jewel-toned flowering bulbs mark the end of winter. They can inspire you to do some of your loveliest arrangements just because they do symbolize the marvel of renewed life.

Take a hint from nature's design. Display slender branches high or at the edges of your grouping. Silhouette them to outline every twig and stem. If bunched together, their beauty is obscured, so prune judiciously to remove all conflicting portions.

Put masses of round and trumpet-shaped flowers low—as though at ground level—for the most dramatic of contrasts.

As flowers drop from branches, green leaves will sprout in striking patterns. You can replace blooms to refresh the arrangement and make it last much longer.

The right container helps

Select a container that's simple and sturdy in character. These spring beauties are at their best in informal arrangements. They are in harmony with earthenware or pottery, and are flattered by a dark tone, or one that takes its color cue from the blooms themselves. For this reason you will be wise to save your crystal and patterned china bowls and vases for more formal arrangements.

Flowering plum with tulips

Beguiling as a pink cloud is this arrangement of flowering plum and rose tulips with their own fresh green foliage. Place 7 branches, 7 tulips in a low container. Cut tallest of your branches twice the length of bowl; slant tip over center

Trailing branches to grace the fireplace mantel

Mantels are ideal spots for flower arrangements, provided that you take account of their somewhat special requirements.

Use a long, low container that won't appear to be in danger of tipping over the edge. Even if you know it *is* safe, it must also *look* safe to be satisfying.

Remember that if you want viewers to see into flower faces, you'll have to place them lower, and turn some out more sharply into the room than in arrangements intended for low tables.

In the bouquet pictured, delicate flowering rose branches (you could substitute forsythia) serve as background. Cut first branch at least 1½ times length of bowl; place to trail over mantel's edge. Arrange four more branches as pictured. Cut yellow tulips various heights; place high, to left. Cluster three red ones low, to right.

Show off spring beauties on your party tea table

With flowering branches, you can afford to break rules concerning height. Here, tallest branch is about three times length of container instead of conventional 1½ or 2 times the length that is usually suggested. Delicacy of line keeps arrangement from having a top-heavy effect.

Red-leafed plum (Prunus pisardi) is the flowering branch used here, but quince or cherry would serve much the same purpose. The branches are pliable enough so you can easily bend them in triangular form as we have done.

With the plum we've used two early double and three single tulips, together with seven narcissus and seven golden daffodils.

Perfume the air and delight the eye with lilac plumes

Lilacs nod above spring bulbs

Completed arrangement includes three narcissus and three tulips, plus six branches of lilac. See pictures and descriptions below of the first steps taken in assembling this spring bouquet

Use lilac branches to define your outline

Three lilac stems are used to establish basic structural lines of this arrangement. The foliage has been stripped from lower parts of branches but left on at the top where it's needed to give the proper fullness

Here, three more of the lilac branches are added to the arrangement. Notice they are cut shorter than the others. Tulips and narcissus, each cut to a different length, add a final touch to the spring array

"Warble me now for joy of lilac time," we sing with Walt Whitman in praise of this fragrant flower. The deep purple of its still-closed bud tips shades off delicately to pale tones at the base of each fresh flower head. Every plume's a color composition in itself.

White and blue lilacs do not have the self-contained color variations of their more traditional purple cousins, but they have more sophistication—a quality that appeals to many. It's easy to imagine a properly placed bouquet of white lilacs bringing a whole room to life.

Should you prefer to use lilacs alone, the flower and its heart-shaped leaves are entirely sufficient. Try an informal arrangement in your silver or pewter water pitcher and see how the sheen of the container en-hances the feathery, soft look of the flowers.

Lilac also performs beautifully in arrangements like the one we show across the page. Combine it freely with bright, spring-flowering bulbs that naturally come into bloom at the same time—tulips, narcissus, daffodils. Add other flowering branches for massed arrangements in the more traditional manner.

Prune well for clean lines

Failure to prune sufficiently is a frequent fault of beginners using lilac branches in arrangements where line is important. Study each branch. Discover its natural curves of beauty. Then prune excess leaves and twigs and place it properly. Don't drown the lilac flowers in a great sea of green leaves.

Keep lilacs from wilting

by preparing them properly

Remove from base of branch all foliage you will not need in your arrangement. Then split end of branch with hammer or cut it crosswise for a distance of an inch or two. Now the branch can freely drink in water to keep it fresh

◄Submerge pounded stem in denatured alcohol for *only* 3 to 5 minutes. Cut to length desired in arrangement and place in fresh water. You'll find this same treatment is equally as effective for all kinds of flowering branches with typically woody stems

Sometimes you will find that blooms spread too far apart to be effective. You can avoid a spindly look by using florists' tape to bring the branches closer together. Be sure to cut lilac branches on a slant so you will be able to insert them easily on a needlepoint holder ►

Branches add rhythmic

Tulips and branches

The rosy hue of tulips and plum blooms is enhanced by the sharp color contrast with a brilliant blue container, its shape repeating round form of tulip blooms. Place needlepoint holder in bottom of vase; insert three flowering branches of various lengths so their outer tips will form a triangle. Place tulips so every flower head will remain quite separate

Featuring rhododendrons

Sturdy Siberian pea shrub with delicate yellow flowers and tiny chartreuse leaves are used to create an airy and springlike background for six rhododendron clusters with their own shiny foliage

Tossed by the winds of spring

Placement of three flowering crab branches suggests motion—as though a wind were moving through them. You could use either needlepoint holder, held firm by florists' clay, or crushed chicken wire to secure. Or, try the Japanese method, using a forked twig, as explained in the section on Oriental style

harmony to flower portraits of spring

Color of china pattern is echoed in flowers for table

Graceful flowering crab and tulips that almost match in hue are arranged in a low, rectangular container whose outer color intensifies flower tones. This is an excellent example of a composition using a red-green color scheme with subtlety

Showy tulips and their foliage are all you'll need

The right container can lend elegance to two tulips

You respond at once to the lovely, curving lines of two tulips because they're placed in a ceramic bud vase whose pleasant curves echo those of stems and leaves. Cut first of two blooms with a stem at least two times the height of the vase; put it in straight and allow to curve naturally. Cut second 1½ times vase height. Slant it toward your left shoulder. Arrange three leaves to follow natural lines of growth and hold blooms in position

Step-by-step procedure for arranging nine tulips

 Put needlepoint holder in corner of oblong bowl. Follow picture and diagram for placement. Cut first tulip 1½ times bowl length; second, ⅔; third, ⅓ height of the first

 Put fourth tulip, ¾ height of the first, to the right and back of the first. Cut the fifth and sixth tulips ⅔ and ⅓ the height of the first and place them as in diagram

*Easy-to-do professional tricks
that help you in arranging tulips*

Tulips are so accommodating a flower, always willing to lend their color to our mixed arrangements, that we may forget how rewarding they can be all by themselves. With nothing more than their own pointed foliage, they'll blazon such color that two—as in the picture at left—can give the effect of many.

Keep to a single color within each arrangement for best result. Or combine the various shades—pale to dark—of one color. Several colors in one group may look spotty.

Florists have tulips for sale in pots and as cut flowers long before your own—if you have a garden—can push their heads up above ground. If prices seem high, remember that forced bulbs will not bloom again. Nor will they if extra-long stems and all of the foliage has been stripped off.

Tips on cutting your own tulips

If you're picking your own tulips, remember to cut most with the shorter stem you'll need anyway—only a few tall ones to give you needed height. Keep some foliage on each bulb, for it is through the leaves that strength is built for next year's bloom.

For tulips from either your garden or the florist's shop, follow our suggestions at right to condition and keep blooms fresh longest.

Keep leaves on tulips for a prettier bouquet. Wrap strip of narrow, green florists' tape around each bloom and give it a quick twist to secure. Do this gently so you won't damage petals. This will hold the tulip closed till you've completed your arrangment. Tulips open up wide so quickly that you'll find them easier to arrange and more effective if blooms are held closed until you put them on display

Wrap the taped tulips snugly in waxed paper or newspaper; leave the paper open at both top and bottom. Fasten with florists' tape to hold flowers in upright position. Put in deep, cold water in a cool, draftless corner for about an hour to let them recover from the shock of cutting before you begin to work with them. Once tulips are conditioned, they'll last longer in *shallow* water than they do deep water

If you find that stems are too weak and won't stand up straight when you begin to arrange your tulips, here's how you strengthen them. Gently insert a No. 22 green florists' wire into each stem at base of the flower head. Then secure wire down farther on stem with bit of florists' tape. When arranging, hide wire with a well-placed leaf. Don't wire every stem; some should curve naturally

Hopkins

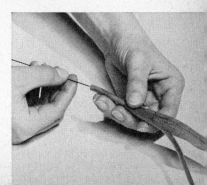

Crooked stems on tulips are apt to break when you try to straighten them with ordinary pressure. Avoid this by carefully inserting No. 22 florists' wire. Start at cut end and use your fingers for supporting stem as wire advances. You can push wire all the way up the stem to flower's head if necessary

Cut seventh flower slightly longer than fifth and place next to fifth tulip. Place last two blooms low, both facing the two tallest flowers. To finish, cover holder with pebbles

Make the most of just a few flowers

Let your spring bouquets be symbolic of the beginning of a new growing cycle. Barren winter has ended, and the burgeoning season—so long awaited—has just begun. We appreciate each new bud and leaf.

In the same way, arrangements for our homes can make a virtue of scarcity. A few flowers at this time of year will give as much pleasure as great armloads can later on, when nature's generous hand supplies us with many flowers and luxuriant foliage.

Sometimes you do need a sizable spring arrangement, appropriate in scale for a large table or a big wall space. When you do, try augmenting a few blooms with large flowering branches as in the arrangement below.

Generous bouquet

from a few tulips

plus long branches

When the first blooms appear on flowering trees or shrubs, bring a few branches inside for a gay bouquet—and fun experimenting with ways to use flowering branches. This is your chance to use long, sweeping lines for a dramatic effect such as the one pictured here.

Let one tall branch soar skyward and a second trail gracefully over the edge of a table. Just a word of caution: you'll need a tall container to give a sense of balance and proportion to your arrangement when you use those long shoots. Some crumpled chicken wire placed inside—if your vase is opaque—will anchor the stems solidly.

Add cut flowers as the focal point of your arrangement. You won't need many. Here a few tulips provide the vital eye-appeal for complete arrangement.

Here are the easy steps to a well-proportioned arrangement

1 Place tallest bloom, 2 times as long as 7-inch bowl, on needle holder. Cut second 10 inches long; slant left. Trim third stem to 9 inches; place low, to right

2 Now cut a daffodil 12 inches long and put it back and left of tallest bloom. Place 8-inch flower directly below tallest one. Include some of the foliage for contrast

What suggests spring so well as a bright grouping of white narcissus and yellow daffodils?

In early spring you may discover you have a few blooms from each of several types of narcissus. By all means cut them—they'll make a lovely arrangement.

Choose a long, shallow container; anchor a needlepoint holder in it with florists' clay, off-center. Now you're ready to begin building your design. Select the tallest stem, with the smallest flower, and cut it 1½-2 times length of your bowl. Now cut the other stems varying lengths, remembering that taller ones should have the smaller blooms and the shorter ones the larger flowers. In the arrangement shown here, yellow, double blooms were the obvious choice for the focal point. Three tulips would make a good substitute for double yellow narcissus. Use some foliage.

You don't need an elaborate holder for a spring bouquet

A pitcher adds a pert touch

Watch the happy smiles when you put a bright bouquet like this on your breakfast table! All it takes are a red tulip, two narcissus, and three graceful sprays of forsythia in milk pitcher from the kitchen shelf

Plain bowl accents beauty of design

Square bowl of light green underscores beautifully balanced triangular line of this arrangement. Smaller blooms are placed straight and high; side clusters slightly forward. Yellow daffodils make focal point

Here's a well-balanced bouquet for your coffee table

A small arrangement isn't overpowered by its setting if it is well balanced. Here the unusual pattern of the glass basket complements the full, red tulips that are the focal point. Three tall quince sprigs give the needed height; the white narcissus spike and broad, curved tulip leaves complete the bouquet for your coffee table

Baskets of spring flowers will brighten any room in your home

Here's a bouquet as fresh and informal as a spring day in a garden. Insert sprays of bleedingheart high and to the back. Put one daffodil low and slanted right to complete triangle design. Next, place white narcissus.

Now put two daffodils below the narcissus. Use early double short-stemmed tulips low, tucking largest in around edge of basket. Single and double tulips are excellent for filler.

When you use a basket, don't bury its handle. Take advantage of its arching line, rough texture for added interest in design.

Tulips and lilacs for Easter

This is an Easter basket the whole family can enjoy. Pink, yellow, and red tulips combine with a lilac stem to frame a giant plastic-foam egg and two rooster heads. If you've a well-designed figurine appropriate to a spring theme, you can use it in a similar manner

You can use some vegetables, too

Lettuce rosettes and well-scrubbed carrots accent colors of flowering-quince, daffodils, and narcissus. Place graceful, curved branch high on needlepoint holder. Use white narcissus to frame basket line. Fill this outline with other materials. Keep the large blooms low

Link branches
and blooms fresh
as spring rains

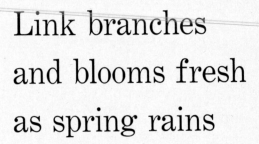

Frame your spring blooms with tall branches of flowering shrubs or new green foliage. Tulips, daffodils, narcissus, and all the host of early flowering bulbs have smooth, bare stems and sculptured individual blooms that make them perfect partners in contrast with lacy patterns of tree and shrub branches.

Always keep flowers to the fore, branches to the back of arrangements which are to be viewed from the front. See how the forsythia branches have been placed in the tall arrangement at left: to give needed height to the grouping, but without hiding the beauty of the narcissus and tulips.

It's quite all right to use several different types of flowers in one arrangement. But do place each type in a small group of its fellows rather than scattered at random.

A spring bouquet that's
right for your tall vase

Cut two branches of forsythia. Let taller one reach straight up. Point second toward your left shoulder. Establish third structural line in bouquet with one red tulip, projecting from vase at rim, pointing toward your right shoulder. Easiest way to anchor this arrangement is by stuffing vase with crushed chicken wire. Insert branches first; tall flowers next; lower ones last

Let lines of branches establish the background

Lines of this arrangement are sketched in with flowering crab branches, cut very early, before the buds had shed their oily, raincoat shells. They are combined with cherry-red tulips in low, rectangular bowl. Large needlepoint holder secures both branches and blooms

A week or ten days later, the branches of flowering crab shown in picture at left have begun to put forth green leaves. Daffodils and iris as well as fresh tulips form the center of interest this time. Notice how flowers of each kind are grouped rather than scattered

---

Take these steps to make cut branches last longer

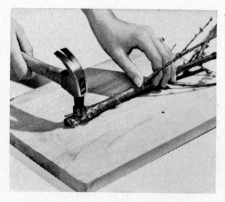

◄ Immediately after cutting the branches, prune away all lowest twigs on main stems. Next, hammer ends of branches until you have split them upward for a distance of two inches

Some Japanese arrangers recommend this step to prevent ➤ wilting: sear end of stem and char bottom two inches of flowering branches with a gas or candle flame or electric burner before you put in water

◄ Quickly place branches in tall can or vase of deep, warm water. Leave them there overnight or at least for several hours. If you put can in a cool, dark corner, it will be easy for branches to drink in water

When you're ready to make ➤ your arrangement, cut branches the lengths desired. Make cuts on a slant so each end will go onto needlepoint holder easily. For thick branches, use clippers to split ends upward

Massive blooms of peonies announce that full summer's almost upon us

Peonies are such fine, big blooms that they demand strong companions in an arrangement, sturdy containers to match their size. Lilac branches and big bearded iris offer excellent contrast of both color and form and hold their own nicely in mixed arrangements such as the two shown on these pages.

Or use the waxy peony by itself, with its own foliage—as in the arrangement of just one bloom which you see across the page. Additional bouquets using peonies alone are shown on pages 92-93.

How to cut and prepare

Peonies may be cut at any time after color shows in the bud and until they reach a fully open stage. Of course, they last longer if not full blown when cut. Leave at least two leaf stems on the stalk to aid in storing up the root strength for next year's blooms.

Scrape and split the stems and condition in deep water for stem strength before making your arrangement. If blooms show signs of wilt, you can usually revive them with 110-degree water, as described on page 66.

Double peonies with flag iris

Iris, because of sharply contrasting color and foliage, are ideal partners for peonies. Used here to lend height, iris are inserted in back of peonies.

Five blooms were chosen carefully to represent a series of stages in development—from partly to fully open. Largest full bloom is placed lowest, in foreground, as focal point in a flower composition which you intend to be seen from the front.

Four spears of iris foliage break the pattern of predominantly round forms of peony blooms. Peony leaves fill spaces between the flower heads.

Maximum effectiveness with a minimum of material is a challenge

Look what you can do with one handsome Chinese peony and five of its own deeply notched leaves!

Place a small needlepoint holder in the bottom of your vase and secure it with florists' clay. Anchor your peony on it, slanted slightly toward the right side.

Now you're ready to insert your leaves. Select and place them so that they form a triangular frame for the single bloom. The peony will help to hold them up if their stems are too short to insert into the holder.

Blue-green of pottery vase is well chosen to blend with foliage and contrast with delicate pink of the flower.

Peonies and lilac branches for a big arrangement to place on floor or platform

Late spring and early summer— when peonies and lilacs bloom—is also a favorite time for weddings. An arrangement like this one (or it could be one of a pair) would make an impressive altar decoration. It would be handsome on any occasion, placed on the floor, if it had plenty of free space around it.

Use a heavy bronze or pottery container, preferably in some dark color, to give a sense of solidity.

Two lilac branches—one lavender, one white—form two points of the triangle. Third point is made by one partly open peony at the lowest point on the right. Fill in center pocket with 14 more peonies, each one cut to a different length.

Revel in color with arrangements of iris

The regal iris comes to us nowadays in so eye-delighting a pallette of colors that one of its varieties is bound to harmonize with your color scheme. Hues range from an almost snowy white to cream and yellow, pink, a nearly-crimson hybrid, and deep purple.

Flag iris—like most of the large singles used in the arrangements pictured on these pages—don't travel. Bring them straight from the garden and arrange at once.

If you have no iris to pick, the Japanese iris which your florist carries for a good portion of each year are considerably less fragile and can be used in similar fashion.

Place iris in a low container

Low bowls or dishes—rectangular, round, or oval—are perfect containers. In them, the iris may be grouped so each bloom will show to perfection.

In general, iris are most appealing in arrangements which focus attention on graceful lines rather than mass effect of bloom. They combine beautifully with such delicate spiky flowers as gasplant, snapdragon, stock, veronica, columbine-leaf, rue, gayfeather, or purple sage.

Some iris foliage looks well in arrangements. But be quite sparing of the amount you cut. If many leaves are cut too short, there may be no blooms the next season.

Use vivid colors for bright accents

Peonies, gasplant, and two varieties of iris are combined in this bouquet with striking effect. Three starry, purple bearded iris form triangular frame for large flag iris and peonies. Two feathery white spikes of gasplant make a pleasing contrast with rounded forms of iris and peonies

Pastel shades are restful and appealing

In this arrangement three dictamnus spikes form a triangular frame for iris. Place deeper-colored iris low; lighter blooms high. You'll have a more interesting arrangement if you'll face all blooms up, and cut each one a different length. Soft meadowrue stalks fill in background, and complete design

Choose colors for your arrangements to accent theme of your next party

The soft, delicate hues of this arrangement hint of bridal showers and festive parties. Arrangement is simple, muted to give full attention to lovely color harmony. The darkest bloom is used as focal point, with the pointed, green iris leaves as accent.

Since this arrangement is constructed for front viewing only, it will be most attractive placed against a wall of harmonizing color, or at one end of your dining table. White container keeps the pastel mood of the arrangement. Leaf pattern of china reflects shape and color of iris leaves.

This flower composition has an arranging trick or two you'll want to copy

Snapdragons form the triangle, iris fill the pocket for this medium-size arrangement, suited to a variety of locations in your home. The glaze lining of this shallow container picks up the color of the yellow iris. Small touches like this add interest and finished appearance to your arrangements, as do the dark stones which cover the needlepoint holder.

Although the snapdragon spikes give an illusion of height to the bouquet, it is still low enough for use on a dining table with some slight modifications of the basic design.

To make a similar arrangement for a dining table centerpiece, you can place additional iris—in the same fashion—on the other side. Each diner should have an equally appealing view of the flowers.

Light up your rooms with peonies

Peonies boast such handsome big blooms and lavish colors, from blush pinks through reddest reds, that they are a joy to bring into the house. But the very generosity of their size—a single flower head is often as big as a saucer—can present some problems.

Scale bouquet size to location

Massiveness of bloom is a proud thing to point to in your garden. But in the home, if space is limited, you must use care not to end with an arrangement that's "outsize."

There are two easy ways to overcome this difficulty: first, use only a few blooms in an arrangement, unless you do have a generous space to fill. Five peonies equal a dozen of most other flowers in bulk.

Second, graduate the stem lengths. Let one or two blooms stand tall; cut others down very short. Place so each bloom can be appreciated for itself.

When you *do* need a large-scale arrangement, peonies can be your best friend. A dozen of them arranged like the glowing pink ones opposite, could light up the room.

Lemon lilies and peonies

Golden hearts of white peonies suggested combining them with lemon lilies. Tallest lily stalk measures 28 inches; others are 26 and 25 inches. Slant largest peony, 12 inches long, to left shoulder, low. Add remaining peonies of different lengths as shown

Bold colors for neutral background

Peonies like these have the vivid, splash color that's perfect against a neutral background. Red blooms are dramatic enough to compete happily with the pattern of the container. Place tallest stem first; arrange four shorter ones below it. Foliage frames lower blooms, accents the tallest, furnishes contrast

A dozen peonies placed to please from any angle

One-color arrangements can be the most dramatic of all if they are handled with subtlety as this one is. Low container reinforces the rosy hue of the blooms with its slightly darker tone. Careful separation of flower heads is the result of cutting the stem of every peony to a different length.

Maximum use is made of the natural contrast between flowers and leaves: flowers are round, somewhat shaggy; leaves are deeply notched and glossy. By concentrating foliage at base of arrangement, the necessary sense of weight to support height is achieved.

Tallest flower—much smaller than those at the base—is cut twice the width of the low bowl. Rest of the blooms—11 more—are cut to different stem lengths so each bloom rises separately from others. All are held in place on a 5-inch needlepoint holder. It's important that holder be big enough. A small one will not hold all the stems securely and is likely to topple over.

Your bouquet's lovelier when it fits the setting

This arrangement of pink peonies and orchid flag iris suits its setting —a sizable occasional table—and retains its importance even with a tray and pitcher in front of it.

When you plan an arrangement, be sure to consider its ultimate location. Small bouquets are lost on massive tables. And a large one's overpowering and slightly ridiculous on a diminutive table.

In this arrangement, necessary height is gained by careful placement of five peonies, while width is provided with three iris. In two-flower arrangements less foliage is used if the color contrast is adequately supplied by the blooms as it is here by pink peonies and blue iris.

Roses announce it's summer

Capture the heady perfume of summer in a bouquet of roses—no matter what the time of year. They're America's favorite flower, and you can have them any time from your florist, as well as from your summer garden.

Just because the desire to smell a rose is universal and irresistible, try to place the bouquet where all can indulge and so reward the sense of smell as well as the eye.

Roses are resplendent in line arrangements with nothing more than their own foliage. And they're also magnificent when massed and combined with spiky or feathery stalks of such plants as delphinium, snapdragons, larkspur, buddleia. Or see how the rosy loosestrife is used in mixed bouquet pictured across the page.

Is there a "right" container?

The old theory that roses, a "fine" flower, *must* be placed only in crystal or silver containers is exploded. Let the degree of formality or informality you want help you decide.

Follow these tips on cutting and conditioning garden roses

Roses should be cut before they reach their peak, then allowed to open indoors. Best time of day is either early in the morning or toward the last hours of daylight—not during the hottest, middle part of the day.

Be sure to use a very sharp knife or pruning shears so you won't crush stems and make it impossible for water to be absorbed. Roses need plenty of water, so this is an important matter if you want your bouquet to last.

Remove lower leaves from the stems; scrape outer bark from bottom half-inch. Condition in deep water, almost up to blooms. Foliage won't be hurt by immersion in water for a few hours.

Cut to get more roses

When you cut a rose, do it with thought of buds to come later as well as health of the bush. Take no longer a stem than needed; shorter-stemmed roses are needed in your bouquet. For more roses from the same stem later on, leave at least two leaves of five leaflets each below the point where you make a cut. New buds will form in axils of the leaves you didn't cut

Mass roses in a mixed bouquet

Rosy loosestrife fashions the background for short-stemmed garden lilies and red roses. Tall center stem forms tip of triangular arrangement. Cut other stems to different, shorter lengths. Face the lily blooms up, toward your shoulder

Take just three roses . . .

If roses are few, you need only three to duplicate this arrangement. The tallest stem should extend from vase at least 1½ times the vase's height. Stagger shorter stems to form triangle. All stems should seem to spring from one point

Hints that help to make bouquets last longer

Get roses off to a good start by snipping stems ⅛ to a full inch while under water. This prevents air blocking minute channels through which water rises in stems. Repeat if you are rearranging a bouquet later on

Roses dislike a draft because fast-moving air robs their petals of moisture too quickly. Don't place bouquet in front of an open window or in path of electric-fan currents. In winter, avoid heat of radiators, hot air registers

Styles in roses—formal or informal

Roses respond well to use in either mass or line arrangements. As a rule, emphasis on line will result in a more informal appearance. Mass effects are generally more formal in character. The two arrangements shown on these pages are good examples of these quite different styles.

In this bouquet just below, the massing of blooms—plus an appropriate container and setting—produces a stately look.

Across the page you see roses placed so stem lines are emphasized, in a low, pottery container. The impression is totally different, though equally agreeable. This is an arrangement that would be at home in modern settings where simplicity's a goal.

Foliage to use with roses

Stay away from asparagus fern or other too delicate foliage. The bloom of the rose is very strong competition and is best with its own leaves or other boldly formed foliage which has definite lines and sharp pattern.

*For a formal setting
use roses and heather
with striking foliage*

Variegated pittosporum foliage, with its whorl-shaped leaves, is placed to form triangular background for this large-scale arrangement with an appealing, old-fashioned air. Nearly full-blown roses are the attention-getting focal point of the composition.

Sprigs of heather introduce a welcome spiky contrast to the predominantly round forms of both blooms and foliage.

Snow-on-the-mountain is one possible alternative to the variegated pittosporum. Or use another bold-leaved variety from the broad-leaf evergreen family to which pittosporum belongs. See foliage lists at end of chapter.

Large, footed china bowl is given additional height by being set on a pedestal. Dainty china figurine placed nearby advances the theme of old-fashioned charm suited to traditional settings.

1 We begin with two Tawny Gold and one New Yorker rose. Tallest stem (should be as near the bud stage as possible) is 18 inches long for a 12-inch, low container. Half-open yellow rose is 12 inches long; red rose 10 inches

2 Now we are ready to add four yellow, half-opened blooms, cut to the following lengths: 17, 16, 14 and 13 inches. Place each one at a gentle slant around center blooms, as pictured. Cut away all of the superfluous foliage

Informal arrangement uses roses of two colors

3 We complete the arrangement by adding four more practically full-blown red roses. Tallest of these last additions— in central position—is 7 inches long; the stems of the other two are 6 and 5 inches respectively. Place so each bloom has a space to itself, and is not crowded.

Notice that the container used is neutral, gray-green on outer surface, yellow inside, in a hue that's close to the Tawny Gold roses. In bouquets combining two colors, choose a container that will remain anonymous.

Lilies are proud beauties

White lilies and their glossy foliage lend themselves to an informal arrangement in a low pottery container

An extremely casual arrangement of Easter lilies, most of them still in bud stage, accompanied by nothing but their own foliage, imitates natural growth patterns. Lilies are allowed to face each other in random fashion.

Total effect is refreshingly unstudied and the arrangement would be well suited to any informal setting. It is low enough so that it could be used as a table centerpiece, as well as on an end table.

Needlepoint holder is placed at the left, rear corner of the low, rectangular bowl. Lilies are inserted so that tip flower of one stalk reaches higher than all the others. Another stalk is placed on an almost horizontal line, emphasizing the shape of the container. Additional lily stalks are placed to fill in angle.

Massed Easter lilies, with ti leaves and chinaberries reflect their gracious setting

This Traditional arrangement was displayed at an exhibit of the Garden Club of Evanston, Illinois, whose theme was "Tradition in Flowers and Furnishings," and reflects the elegance of the yellow Venetian brocade drapery and the Elizabethan oak dower chest that formed its setting.

The dark, polished ti leaves boldly outline the star-shaped Easter lilies, and the branches of chinaberry, cascading over the rim of the round pewter bowl, add a softening touch. The use of the smaller berry clusters behind them is, of course, optional. Here, they provide color contrast.

Several other plant materials could be substituted. Canna leaves could serve as the background and some high-bush cranberry clusters for the chinaberry used here.

Contrast handsome lilies with cool blue delphinium spikes for an impressive arrangement

There is a formal feeling about this arrangement of blue delphiniums and gold-touched lilies which invites pause and relaxation. The metallic-blue and copper-green basic-type container is Japanese pottery. A few proud containers are a better investment than a large assortment of undistinguished ones, even if initial price seems a bit steep.

Form the triangular background of delphiniums by trimming the tallest stalk to about twice the diameter of the bowl and placing it on the rear of a large needlepoint holder. Cut a second stalk three-fourths the length of first and slant it slightly to the left. Third stem is three-fourths the length of the second and it slants to the right. Fill in design with other flowers of varying lengths.

For contrast of form and weight at the base of the composition, lilies are a good choice; they flower at about the same time as the first delphinium spikes.

Lift zinnias to elegance by combining them with lovely red-flecked lilies

This arrangement skillfully combines everyday zinnias with sophisticated lilies for an effect that's satisfying to the most conservative arrangers.

Here these slender-stemmed lilies, buds as well as fully open, form an airy background for the large, round zinnias. Tallest lily stem is cut two-and-one-half times the length of the bowl. A second lily and long-stemmed zinnia complete the triangle. The zinnias are in shades of red and white, mirroring the colors of the lilies, and the two small white ones, reaching far to the right, balance the height of the lily stalks in the background.

If *your* reasons for making unusual flower combinations are equally sound, by all means, do so. There are no unbreakable rules in arranging flowers— that's why it's an art, not a science.

Arrangements that interpret summer

Summer's free and easy mood, her fullness, color, and generally extravagant ways ought to inspire us when we design bouquets appropriate to this luxuriant season.

There's more than one way to imitate summertime at her height. Most obvious, of course, are those generous—almost overwhelmingly generous—effects we can achieve in mass arrangements that are reminiscent of nature at her most lavish.

Another more subtle way of capturing summer's spirit with flowers is to emphasize the informal curves and spreading lines characteristic of midsummer growth. They are quite different from the spear shapes that denote spring, or the sparse, thin lines most typical of autumn.

The two arrangements on this page take advantage of the naturally loose and spreading lines of summer growth. Copy them by using both buds and fully opened flowers, just as they grow on a plant. Fuller arrangements on opposite page echo generosity of the season in ample use of plant materials.

Use plenty of cool, green nasturtium foliage with the "hot" oranges, golds, and scarlets of the flowers. Arrange with lots of buds among the wide-open blooms. Buds will continue to open and keep arrangement interesting longer. Gain height and breadth for the composition by twining long nasturtium stems around sticks; place as tall back and right horizontal lines. Group short blooms at center

Petunias are pretty in a pitcher
that emphasizes free-flowing lines

Petunias grow so plentifully all summer long that you won't mind cutting some to bring indoors when the growing season is at its height. They're an informal flower, so use them in a free and easy style that seems natural. Tallest stem is two and one-half times height of pitcher, placed at center back. Establish the main outlines of your arrangement first. Then fill in "holes" with the shorter-stemmed blooms. Select flowers of closely related colors to get the most pleasing effect

Proper conditioning is necessary for poppies

Oriental poppies, with their appealingly fragile and paper-thin petals *can* be used successfully in bouquets if you treat them properly.

Pick them the night before bloom opens; sear stem ends immediately after cutting. Use a candle or gas flame to sear. This prevents sticky fluid in stems from escaping. Condition the poppies in deep water overnight before arranging.

In the morning, when bloom is fully open, put a drop of wax in heart of flower to keep it open. This will considerably prolong life of your arrangement since poppies usually close at the end of a day.

Feathery meadowrue furnishes the background for this graceful line composition. Notice that each poppy stem is cut to a different length, slanted to separate blooms.

Studied informality in the French fashion

Marie Antoinette — who liked to dress herself and her court ladies as elegant shepherdesses — would have approved of this romantic midsummer bouquet.

An antique French vase, of a cornucopia shape, decorated with coy shepherdess and lamb, dictated the basic outline.

Wild penstemon (branches of almost any fine-leaved shrub are a possible substitute) establishes taller background lines.

Masses of primroses of several varieties make up the central portion. The meadowrue, columbine, floribunda fairy roses and auricula are placed casually at the right and upper edges of the arrangement, softening outline.

Other flowers of shape similar to primroses which might handily be substituted for them are: anemones or campanula.

Try daylilies for versatility

Daylilies are just what their name implies —they're lilies that bloom for only one day. They flourish in sunlight but they close at night. Consequently you'll do well not to use them in an arrangement you want to look its best at night, unless you're careful to pick some stems with buds that will open as the full blooms fade.

But don't let this quirk frighten you! Daylilies bloom prolifically all summer and are versatile combined with other flowers—as you can see from pictures taken at a meeting of the National Hemerocallis Society. (Hemerocallis is the daylily's botanical name.)

Daylilies mirror copper

Rich apricot daylilies tipped with red make a striking arrangement with wild butterfly weed, clematis vine. Simple copper pitcher is the vase ➡

Daylilies and wild vervain

Daylilies combine beautifully with light, airy flowers. Five stems of gray-leaved wild vervain make the background for the clusters of amber and yellow daylilies. Put light ones high, deeper ones low, facing upward

Here's a formal bouquet

Be lavish with garden flowers! Try a bouquet in the grand manner, with the pyramid centered with golden daylilies and outlined with rust ones

Here's a striking arrangement you can copy. Wild sunflowers balance the hemerocallis in a copper-scale-pan flower bowl. Use a shallow liner pan to hold water. Garden amaryllis leaves form the fan-shaped background, which radiates from an ear and tassel of corn. This will add a bright note to your console

Three branches of rosy crabapple—tall enough to balance the high container—make a triangular frame for the brown-eyed Susans and the henna-toned daylilies. The jar is brown pottery—simply designed so that it won't compete with the blooms

A successful arrangement will create a mood to blend with its location. The one pictured would be a good accent for a smart, Modern room. The velvety sumac berries and the stark branches add interest to this unusual grouping of wine-red hemerocallis. The sturdy stone jar and the slab of bark add a rugged touch

Giant yellow daylilies feel and look like exquisite mandarin silk. Black-red hazel leaves add a vivid color contrast, give a sophisticated air that is ideal with the plain, Modern vase; makes a showy grouping for your mantel, the bookcase, or the hall table

Zinnias and marigolds can star for you

It's easy to take zinnias and marigolds for granted because they're so common in summer gardens. Don't do it. They can be the flower arranger's best friends, not only because they bloom all season but because they mimic other blooms—such as chrysanthemums and dahlias—so well in size and texture that you won't tire of using them.

Handle them with care, but don't hesitate to prune foliage as much as necessary, using it only for accents.

1 Cut first zinnia twice length of bowl. Put just back of center on needlepoint holder. Cut second ⅔ height of first; slant left. Cut the third ½ height of first; slant right

2 Fill in triangle. Cut fourth an inch longer than second; place back of first. Place a fifth zinnia, an inch shorter than third, center front, facing toward the first flower

Zinnias are the obvious choice when you want to fill an earthenware jug with flowers. Their bold colors, rough texture balance such containers perfectly. Place tallest stem, with partially opened bud, high; largest flowers low. Cut others different lengths and fill in the design

3 Slant sixth flower, an inch shorter than second so it stands between first and second. Cut last zinnia an inch shorter than sixth. Face it to the back and to right

These arrangements are attractive from any viewing angle

A bouquet that is lovely from any angle is the right accent for your dining table or on a coffee table. Here a triangle of marigolds is highlighted by five large, orange zinnias, each one cut a different length so that the individual blooms remain separated. Lacy foliage of marigolds provides needed contrast in both color and shape to the flower forms

Turn the glass basket around, and you'll see an arrangement of marigolds as attractive as the one on the other side! Triangular design is maintained by substituting large blooms for the zinnias. Note buds of marigolds are used in this arrangement as contrast to large, bright blooms. Use stem with at least one bud as your tallest, cutting it 1½ times width of container. Trim largest blooms short for the base

A bouquet of zinnias and marigolds that's pretty, any way you look at it

Cut highest zinnia 22 inches long. Put in rear center. Slant 15-inch zinnia to right shoulder; 13-inch one to left. Put 19-inch stem to right and back of tallest zinnia. Fifth one, 8 inches long, points to you, slanting from low center front.

Face blooms up. Sixth zinnia is 16 inches long. Place at slight slant to left of tallest bloom. Cut next 14 inches long and slant right and back of tallest. Put eighth flower (12 inches) in front of highest, at angle facing you.

In front add 11-inch zinnia pointing right, a 10-inch stem near far left one. 6-inch stem goes back of 10-inch bloom. Turn bowl around. Cut four zinnias and five marigolds varying lengths. Fill in triangle to complete unity of the design.

You can sketch bold outlines using glads

Visualize your arrangements
before you place a single flower

Successful arrangements never "just happen." This one looks simple, but it was constructed with careful attention to growth lines of the flower to determine the position that would express its greatest beauty. The tall, center stalk balances the height of the vase. The two shorter ones, slanting left and right, complete the triangular design; a large, full bloom, placed just above the rim of the vase, slightly forward, softens the contrast between container and plant material

Arrangements should be
an integral part of
their background and setting

When you place an arrangement near a painting or a print, be sure it belongs there. You gain nothing if the bouquet dwarfs your picture, or if its colors distract the viewer.

This one is appropriate to its setting because it echoes the Oriental mood of the Japanese print and is in complementary scale. The tall gladiolus stem, placed on the rear of the needlepoint holder, represents heaven line of an Oriental arrangement. Two graceful, arching stems, slanting to right and left, sketch in the base of the triangle, and the additional stems, trimmed to different lengths, fill in the design. Use a few leaves for contrast.

Try these tips to condition your gladiolus before arranging

Cut your glads when the second floret is ready to open. Recut each of the stems just before you place it in deep water. Allow ample space for each bud to expand petals. To avoid having all stiff, straight stems, lean some stalks slantwise during conditioning period. Tiny buds at tips seldom open and may be removed at the start, unless needed for height

Glads stimulate the arranger's imagination

*Five blooms can be as
impressive as a dozen
in bouquets like this*

A gladiolus arrangement doesn't have
to be massive. A few full blooms and
some bud tips make an artful bouquet
for a table. Place upright stem, with
three florets, in the center of your container. Put one tapering stem, with a
few buds showing color, to the left, just
above the rim of the bowl, and a third
to the right, for a long, horizontal line
in sharp contrast to the globelike bowl.
Use their swordlike leaves for accent.
A ball of crumpled chicken wire or
hardware cloth stuffed into the bowl
will anchor the stems firmly in position

*Emphasize the lines of the
gladiolus in a simple,
easy-to-arrange bouquet*

This bouquet dramatizes the curved
and straight lines that make gladiolus so interesting to arrange. The
tallest stem, with short, graceful tip,
goes in the center of a round bowl.
Curve stem with longest tip slightly
and place it to the left in horizontal
line. Put shorter stem, with partially
opened buds, on the right, opposite
the second. Fill in the center of the
design with shorter glad spikes, cut
varying lengths. You can repeat the
pointed lines of the tips with a few
slender leaves placed to fill in design

1 Before arranging gladiolus stalks, you may want to prune some of the undeveloped bud tips. Place a 24-inch glad in the center of a 12- to 14-inch low bowl. Slant a 16-inch spike to your right and an 8-inch one toward your left shoulder

2 Put 14-inch glad just to left of tall center stalk to disguise its bare stem, and a 7-inch stem low in center, projecting forward over edge of container. Add several foliage spears to each glad for color and line accents. Insert leaves to follow the angles of the flowers nearest them for natural-looking arrangement

3 Now you are ready to put the finishing touches on the arrangement by placing a 20-inch glad to the rear right of the tallest stem to give an illusion of depth to the design. An 18-inch stem goes in front of the tallest spike and slants to the left. When arranging stalks with many blooms, don't crowd them. Make each ruffled flower show.

With this type of arrangement, the low rectangular container has become as "basic" as a black dress in a woman's wardrobe. This irregularly striped one adds a note of contrast to the vertical lines of this design, but a glass baking dish can be used with equal distinction.

Follow this formula as often as you like—each result will be pleasingly varied

Explore woods and roadsides for offerings of fall

Autumn, when the blooms of your garden may be sparse, is the time to open your eyes to new materials for your arrangements. Explore the woods and roadsides. You'll discover a variety of vines of unusual appeal, seed pods, weeds, and grasses, many of them useful and effective in autumn arrangements because of their decorative shapes, colors, and textures. Milkweed pods, sumac, pine cones, oats, cattails, and goldenrod will all add interest to imaginative fall designs.

The weeds, grasses, and cattails in this arrangement can be found on the banks of ponds and marshes. Fill your husband's fishing creel with your discoveries and put it on the end of your dining table the next time he brings home a catch of fish. Pay tribute to his skill with yours

Morning-glories bring color and unusual line patterns to an informal fall table setting

You'll want to try morning-glories in your fall arrangements, before the first frost ends their bloom. Their long, trailing vines and scattered flowers make a graceful silhouette for an informal setting. Let one of the sprays curve to the table. Here the tall, Oriental basket, with a glass liner for water, is balanced by the height of the long tendrils of morning-glory vines.

Before you begin arranging morning-glories, char the ends of the vines over a low flame and plunge them into cold water.

Put a ball of crumpled chicken wire or hardware mesh in the vase and insert the stems in it to hold the arrangement securely.

Bittersweet, with its orange and red accents, is an obvious choice for a fall bouquet. Use it as it grows, keeping your arrangement sharply etched with graceful high and low lines by pruning branches judiciously. Cluster short pieces at the center and sides of a wall holder for a bright spot of color

Here's another interesting wall arrangement. Clip a few sprays of Sweet Autumn clematis and place them in a shellacked gourd or other container with an intriguing shape. Let the vines trail naturally upward and down. They're stiff enough to hold their positions without need of additional propping

Combine grasses, leaves, vines, toadstools, flowers, and driftwood for a distinctive design

You can construct a miniature landscape and add a new vista to your dining table with a number of unusual plant materials.

A design that suggests a field and forest has been created by grasses, caladium leaves, geranium and myrtle vines, chrysanthemums, and a piece of weathered driftwood. The variety of textures, shapes, and sizes they provide creates a number of intriguing and unusual contrasts.

First, place piece of driftwood so that it doesn't crowd your table setting. Put a 4-inch cupped needlepoint holder behind the driftwood and arrange the grasses, white caladium leaves, and garden chrysanthemums on it. Cluster of fungus forms a bridge to the lower half of the arrangement.

On this section, put flat lichen on small needlepoint holders and let graceful, trailing vines, secured in another cupped needlepoint holder, entwine them.

Chrysanthemums—autumnal favorite

Time-honored chrysanthemums were cultivated in China more than 2,000 years ago. The Japanese adopted the flower, developed it highly, and made it officially theirs by incorporating it into the crest and seal of the Mikados, some centuries ago. In Japan of today, it is the prescribed flower, used with pine, to mark joyful New Year celebrations.

A long-lasting flower

Chrysanthemums as cut flowers last so well that they're a deserved favorite for home arrangements. Prepare stems as we suggest on the following pages. They'll reward you by staying fresh for a surprisingly long period, especially small pompon varieties.

Let the type of mum you're arranging be one of the deciding factors when you're selecting an appropriate design and the container. Giant, mop-headed mums of the sort we associate with football games and crisp, autumn weather won't take to the same style of arrangement as the button-tips which you see so effectively used in the mass arrangement pictured below.

Medium-size mums—like those in the low bowl across the page—lend themselves well to line arrangements, *provided* their foliage is fresh and green. Stems minus leaves look bare. When foliage wilts, cut the stems down, rearrange, and combine with other foliage.

Chrysanthemums and dahlias in the opulent style of early Victorian refinement

When a setting for a bouquet speaks so eloquently of one particular period as this one does, it's a challenge to the imagination to select a container and style of arrangement attuned to the surroundings.

Pleasant memories of Victorian charm come to life in the pink and mauve massed arrangement of button mums and dahlias nestled in a Vieux Paris porcelain basket.

Arrangements that are to be placed before a mirror must be skillfully handled to be attractive from back as well as front, since a mirror will reflect the view which is otherwise hidden from our eyes.

In a pierced container such as this porcelain basket, you must, of course, slip in a bowl deep enough to hold water and big enough to take a sizable needlepoint holder.

Dahlias placed at the center of the bouquet serve both as a focal point of interest and to disguise somewhat the basket handle. Leaving the handle completely exposed would divide the arrangement in two.

Stems show to good advantage in this line arrangement of mums in the Oriental manner

Medium-size double mums are far too often thrust into a vase, fluffed out a bit, and passed off as a flower arrangement. If you have indulged in this "easy way out," just because the thin stems and comparatively small flower heads seemed difficult to handle in other ways, let this arrangement inspire your next adventure with mums.

The one prerequisite to success for this type of arrangement is that stems have sufficient foliage, and that it be in perfectly fresh condition. Bare stems or wilting foliage will ruin the effect you want to achieve.

To duplicate this arrangement, begin by establishing three main lines with single stems and blooms. First, insert tallest stem at the back; next add shorter stems to right and left, pointing each forward toward your right and left shoulders.

Next add flowers to gain sufficient fullness for the three major lines. Be sure to graduate stem lengths. Use care not to allow visible stems to crisscross each other.

Last step: fill in center pocket with shortest-stemmed blooms, facing them forward.

Two covered glass jars make unusual containers for mums and huckleberry

Queen of autumn flowers, the giant mum blends happily with huckleberry foliage which is almost universally available from your florist, and inexpensively priced.

Three mums, plus foliage, are adroitly combined as if in a single arrangement, although two containers have been used to achieve a bold effect. Gleaming glass lids are displayed as a part of the composition, and are balanced by the placement of the Oriental figurine at left.

Huckleberry can be manipulated to some extent to assume the curving lines needed for this arrangement. However, it is wise to select large, full branches, then prune away all nonconforming portions of foliage to secure a pattern you want.

Aim for simplicity when mums are few

Ever think of combining short-stemmed chrysanthemums and tawny barberry?

Chrysanthemums, golden colored and so refreshingly aromatic, are worth consideration in a new setting with barberry sprigs, just turning red and yellow. The informality of short-stemmed mums calls for the simplest of containers. Here, large glass ashtray has been used, its smooth lines contrasting pleasantly with shaggy blooms and crisp leaves

Cut stems to lengths you want in your arrangement. Pull off leaves that would be underwater. Crush ends of stems with hammer so the flowers will get water easily

Burn the crushed stem ends until they're black. Perennial mums often have hard, woody stems you can split up from 2 to 5 inches, depending upon how long they are

If petals show signs of falling, seal them around the base with drops of candle wax. Unless they are sealed this way, other petals on the bloom will fall, too

Spider mums shown here are often seen in old Chinese works of art. For arrangements in cylindrical vases, make main outline of "anchor" flowers in your hand and wire them securely. Hold in mouth of vase with left hand and place stems to be used as filler with your right

A sweeping background for a cluster of small mums in a shallow container is provided by Scotch broom, which is easy to manipulate and good for use in arrangements requiring well-defined lines. With informal arrangements, appropriate figurines can heighten the interest

Capture fall's zesty mood with chrysanthemums

Chrysanthemums are as typical of autumn as falling leaves and the tangy smell of bonfires. Here several varieties—spider, daisy, pompom and the large, fluffy Japanese—in brilliant shades of yellow and bronze bring the season's zestful mood to their table settings. In addition, they're long lasting and adaptable to various styles of arrangements.

A shaggy spider mum forms the center of interest in this arrangement for a coffee table. While placing the small, medium and large mums, turn container as you work so that design will be pleasing from every angle. You can gain vivid color contrast by using a bright red bowl similar to this disc-shaped one with yellow flowers

Chrysanthemums give your table a Midas touch

Two of autumn's most captivating colors are combined in this vibrant table setting.

These shaggy mums have been placed low, in a shallow white bowl to encourage cross-table conversation—a very important consideration in the planning of table centerpieces.

Lacy evergreen branches extend the basic design of this arrangement and provide interesting contrasts of shape, color and form with flowers.

Candles always add a festive touch, but make them an integral part of your centerpiece, not just an awkwardly placed afterthought to a table setting.

Here they give needed height interest for the arrangement, and their holders, which match the china dinnerware, serve to unify the entire table setting.

Welcome your guests with a gold-toned autumn centerpiece

You tell your guests you're glad they came when you have a festive centerpiece on the table.

Every detail in the setting shown here has been carefully planned. The flowers have been placed so that some are in profile for a pleasing view from all sides; all are kept low so that they aren't a barrier to dinnertime conversation.

The rich gold and orange mums complement the bright turquoise dinnerware, and the brass bowl and the candlestick holders reflect the golden tones of the flatware. Lighted candles add a soft glow to the setting. And, although the centerpiece has three parts, it is in perfect proportion, occupying only a third of the table length—a good ratio to remember when you are planning table arrangements.

Set a mood with your centerpiece

This centerpiece echoes the mood of the hunter on a crisp, fall morning. Weathered driftwood forms the base for the arrangement. The tall grasses placed in the background sketch in the outline of the duck blind. Small mum cluster gives color accent, while the cattail grouping and the Oriental bronze duck at the far right add to the realism

Accessories can be important, too

When your dinnerware is plain and your setting casual, bring your table to life with a centerpiece that sets a mood. Here two small, square mirror plateaus, reflecting two glass birds, turn a homey pot of ivy and a few tawny pompom mums into a decorative table arrangement

Gather autumn's gift of berried branches

Emphasize satisfying curves

Bittersweet vine goes sophisticated in a striped ceramic vase. Select three long berried sprays with strong curves to establish structural lines. Add shorter sprigs for fullness, focal interest at the center

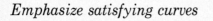

An arrangement of bittersweet and mums in a ceramic coffee container makes the most of exposed wooden handle by reversing and enlarging its curve with tallest stem. This floral design is by Carl Starker

Firethorn's glowing red berries are enhanced by polished Chinese pewter

Berried branches are stereotyped by some arrangers as informal material, and never used in any other fashion. This arrangement demonstrates that so narrow a view is mistaken.

Here, a container and accessories of importance, plus proper handling of the firethorn branches make a harmonious total effect. Central cluster of larger berries is holly, with no foliage showing.

Inspired by, but not adhering closely to the Oriental three-point style, the design is of roughly triangular shape. Chinese pewter container — its lid included in the composition — is an echo of the Far-Eastern influence.

Scarlet coat of mounted soldier in porcelain figurine imitates brilliant color of berries and establishes relationship to grouping, though it is not of Oriental design.

This arrangement, placed on a highly polished antique chest, was seen at the "Tradition in Flowers and Furnishings" show, presented by the Garden Club of Evanston, Illinois.

Highbush cranberry branches with two spikes of gladiolus

1 Tallest branch, 2½ times length of bowl, is placed back of center on holder. Second one, ⅔ height of first, points toward right shoulder. Slant third (½ height of first) low — to left shoulder. Add fourth, same height as third, back of tallest. Fill in with smaller branches

2 Now that background of branches is complete, you're ready to add two spikes of gladiolus to serve as central interest of your arrangement. Cut first spike ½ the height of the tallest branch. Cut second one 3 inches shorter. Slant both at same angle as branch pointing right

Dry flowers for winter color

Fresh flowers and greens—such as goldenrod, strawflowers, cockscomb, oats, rye, leaves, seed pods and ferns—can be dried for rich winter bouquets. You need no special equipment. A closet or your attic can serve as the "drying room," and some of the loveliest materials are found growing wild. Mrs. Louise B. Fisher of Williamsburg, Virginia designed the arrangements shown on these pages and devised the drying instructions as well.

Cut materials at the right times

Cut flowers in semibud form. They'll open into full bloom as they dry. Gather grasses and ferns in the morning when they're fresh. Cut leaves as they start turning from green to yellow and red. Select flat branches.

Put materials for drying in buckets of water as they're cut, if you have to transport them any distance. The sooner you press colored materials after picking, the brighter they'll stay during the drying process.

Dry them in a dark, dry spot

Any dampness will prevent proper drying and light will fade colors. Hang straight-stemmed materials in bunches, heads down (see picture on opposite page). For curved stems, dry in kegs, jars, or bottles. Leaves and grasses must be carefully pressed on a flat, paper-covered surface. Lay them down one layer deep so spines or backs face up and do not overlap. Pile up as many layers as you like, covering each layer with paper. Lay a weight on top. Drying takes from 2 to 4 weeks.

Make brilliantly colored dried bouquets in colonial style

See how much color you can have from dried bouquets? This one combines beech leaves, red sage, goldenrod, cockscomb, golden celosia, blue sage, pearly everlasting. After flowers and leaves are dry and their colors have "set," they won't fade, even if the arrangement is placed in a very sunny spot

Dried flowers, ferns, grasses, and leaves for a mass bouquet

Only dried materials—yellow and rose strawflowers, beech leaves, grasses, fern fronds, honesty, and everlasting—are used in this arrangement in the traditional Williamsburg manner. A massive background is made entirely of leaves, grasses, and ferns, while the center of interest is provided by the bright strawflowers grouped together.

Your dried materials are ready for arranging when the petals feel rigid and no moisture is left in the paper layers. If they're not thoroughly dry when you take them from your presses, leaves will curl. You can store dried materials by covering them with paper sacks or boxes to keep them dust-free until you are ready to use them in your wintertime bouquets.

Here's how to dry fresh flowers and foliage

Press leaves carefully between layers of paper on a flat surface — such as the floor or a broad board. Weight with rug, books, suitcase, or any other handy, heavy object

You will want some curved stems for more interesting arrangements. Dry tall grasses and greens in kegs, fruit jars or milk bottles, placed on the floor of your "drying room." Leave them undisturbed for several weeks

Hang bunches of material that you want to dry with straight stems on lines strung in a dark, very dry room. You can cut the stems later into the different lengths you need

Dried materials alone, or with fresh flowers

Stretch your flower budget with dried foliage

You can supplement a few fresh flowers with dried materials for decorative arrangements during the winter months. Here plumes of pampas grass make a soft, feathery background for six flame glads. Two broad, dried castor-bean leaves contrast with the slender bud tips and leaves, balance upward stretching outline

Combine dried materials with driftwood, rocks

1 Fasten driftwood on large needlepoint holder. Place on block of plywood or plastic foam

2 Cut dried wild parsnip different lengths; secure triangular cluster to right with clay

3 Secure artichoke or thistle seed pods and the eucalyptus twigs to left on a small holder

4 Use rocks to hide holders. Fill in design at right with more artichoke, thistle seed pods

Dried materials have been popular with arrangers since colonial days

The practiced arranger develops a "seeing eye" for beauty in every growing thing. The grasses, weeds, seed pods, and weathered woods the casual observer might reject as too prosaic to be used in a flower arrangement are precious "finds" for the arranger. In this, he is no different from his colonial forebears. Winter bouquets made of dried materials were common in Williamsburg and Mount Vernon.

The arrangement pictured here, of seed heads, leaves, branches and berries, is entirely appropriate to its traditional setting of rich antiques — the mahogany "brothers'" desk, quaint Bristol green glass paperweight, small bronze statuette, the glass study lamp, and the background of framed racing handkerchiefs and Early American prints. Arrangement was displayed at an exhibit of the Evanston, Illinois Garden Club.

Dried mullein head, cut when young, catches the eye immediately in this arrangement designed by Dorothy H. Gleason. A curved piece of weathered wood forms its graceful "leaves," a dried sweetpea vine sketches in height lines

Dried hydrangea blooms serve as the center of interest in an arrangement any beginner can duplicate. Well-pruned dried foliage frames blooms in a graceful triangular design. Stems of materials can be inserted directly in painted block of plastic foam which serves as holder and base for the arrangement

Miniatures that cost little more than imagination

Re-create a scene from nature for a long-lasting winter arrangement

This miniature Oriental scene, suggesting a temple retreat, is made by cementing a weathered grapevine to a cross section of a root. Peruvian moss provides its foliage; try clusters in various positions, varying small, medium, and large ones for natural effects, before gluing to the vine. Complete realistic scene with Oriental figures. Add some stones to give stability and weight

Soft gray-green tones of eucalyptus flower heads combine artfully with the muted tans and browns of date-palm stems, tropic seed pods, lichen, and driftwood to form a tiny wind-swept landscape. The dried materials are secured to base of plastic foam or wood with linoleum-cement glue. Small stones hide arranger mechanics and unify design

Cardinals perch in a silvered sumac tree

A few sprigs of well-pruned sumac on a needlepoint holder form a graceful tree for two cardinal figurines and a tiny nest. Cover holder with cinders and spray with canned snow

*This little snowball tree
is fun for a child to make*

To make this snowball tree, fasten 2½-foot gnarled branch to wood block or heavy needle-point holder. Spray lightly with canned snow and dot with plastic foam snowballs and tiny horns or bows. Small figure will add whimsey

Keep your miniature arrangements simple and clear-cut to show pleasing contrasts between the different shapes of materials you include. Here, the palm scroll provides the height and rhythm to balance a solid block of plastic that acts as a base. Seated Oriental figure sets a mood of repose

Coconut palm spathe holds sprays of sea oats in a moss-disguised needlepoint hold-er. Dried canna leaves provide contrast in texture. Arrangement is a true minia-ture, making an ideal gift for a shut-in

A crab, assorted seashells, sponges, coral, and stones are all mounted on a plastic foam base and combined in an arrangement which depicts life under water. The base could be sprayed with color, or covered with glue and then rolled in sand to give it a more natural appearance. Place the dried branch forward to get a more three-dimensional effect

Arrangements of foliage alone have a fresh look

Shiny-leaved huckleberry has a luxury look that belies its budget price and ready availability. Use it generously in a flamboyant arrangement of sweeping lines to grace a mantelpiece. Two covered jars in which foliage is arranged are treated as a unit

Nothing does more than cut green foliage to freshen up a room at minimum expenditure of both time and money.

Foliage arrangements have a natural affinity for Modern furnishings, Contemporary architecture. But they take to Traditional surroundings also, if they're styled properly and placed in a suitable container.

Foliage is easy to come by: explore the countryside or your own back yard looking for branches of interesting form, and leaves of many shapes, colors. Put them together in double-quick time, enjoy them for weeks.

Aristocratic magnolia foliage holds its own in the most elegant of surroundings. Wipe each leaf and make it shine before arranging branches. This will heighten natural contrast between patent-leather face of leaves and the furry-brown undersurfaces

As proof that foliage arrangements can be tailored to suit Traditional surroundings equally as well as Modern, we show you sedge, pittosporum, and magnolia leaves in a silver urn on a Biedermeier commode. The arrangement was shown at an exhibit of Evanston Garden Club

Imagination and the right vase lend canna leaves a brand-new sophistication

To the ardent flower arranger, nothing's more fun than to use an old and familiar leaf or flower in a clever new way. If you've never thought of hardy canna leaves as potential material for an exotic arrangement, this picture should convince you that it's worth experimenting with.

An iridescent quality in the leaves was considerably heightened by glazed finish of ceramic vase used here.

Canna leaves are pliable and may be manipulated. To get leaves to curve to right and left, bend gently at point where leaf springs out of stem.

In winter, when canna leaves aren't available, try ti leaves—widely sold in florist shops—in a similar manner. They're much the same size and shape as canna leaves, and available in purplish tints as well as in solid green.

Bold, leathery ficus leaves (rubber plant) make an appropriate decoration for a coffee table. This arrangement uses just five leaves in a low container. Fill in with pebbles to conceal the needlepoint holder from view. Leaves are very long lasting if kept in water

Add a welcome green spot to the corner of your writing desk with an arrangement of dieffenbachia leaves. Or make one as a gift for an office-worker friend. It takes only seven leaves, arranged in whorl fashion on a needlepoint holder to duplicate this foliage design

Take just three brilliant red carnations, a few fern fronds, some sprays of variegated holly, a piece of driftwood. Put them together so the holly gives height, the ferns width, and the carnations a glowing spot of color at base of centrally placed driftwood. Display on buffet or table

Fresh-cut greens are winter's jewels

Get acquainted with the evergreen family and use it frequently in winter arrangements —not just at the holidays. Try both piny-fragrant needled types and polish-shiny hollies, magnolia or camellia.

Many of these greens are inexpensive to buy at the florist shop. Almost all are so long lasting you'll feel your money's well spent.

The secret of keeping greens fresh looking for a long time lies in proper preparation of stems. Follow methods for woody branches given earlier in this chapter. Consult checklist of foliage on following pages for new ideas on greens you can use in arrangements.

Greens and berried branches complement each other in a long-lasting arrangement

Here's an arrangement you could make from the lower branches cut off a too-tall Christmas tree. Lightly spray a few of the evergreen branches with canned snow for a frosty look. Leave the rest in their natural green state for pleasing variety and contrast.

Add color interest with brightly berried branches. These are of possumhaw (Ilex decidua), but firethorn would be equally as effective with greens.

Simple container of polished copper is in keeping with the informal character of greens and berried branches. You'll probably have to use more than one needlepoint holder to secure an arrangement as large as this one. Keep dish well filled with water to delay needle drop from evergreen branches.

Miniature arrangement on lower shelf uses evergreen sprigs and one red carnation riding in a four-wheeled buggy.

Use gilded magnolia leaves with greens

Feathery, long-needled evergreen sprigs fashion a wintertime centerpiece. Gilded magnolia leaves, centered with gold tree ornaments add a luxury look. Two white pillar candles of different lengths complete arrangement. Be sure to fireproof greenery

Sprigs of holly set the Christmas scene

Give a fresh background of holly to a treasured figurine that your family likes to put on display each Christmas. Insert the sprigs in a cupholder and fill with water to keep holly green

Two pine branches frame seven short-stemmed roses

1 Cut taller pine branch 1½ to 2 times length of bowl; cut second ⅔ height of first. Rose stem is ½ height of second branch. Place it as shown

2 Cut three more roses and place as shown. Insert the tallest rose to follow stem line of tallest branch of pine. Slant others to the right and left

3 Cut remaining three roses different lengths, all shorter than the ones already placed. Use them to fill in center pocket made by other roses

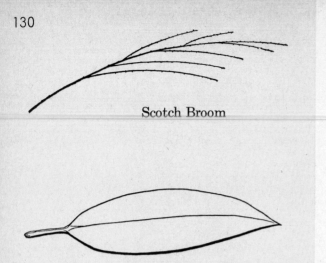

Scotch Broom

Ti Leaf

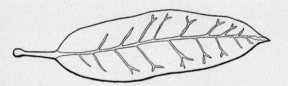

Huckleberry

Croton

Salal

Handy check list of

Choose these from florist's array

A fascinating variety of foliage can be found at the florist's—sold as cut greens or as small inexpensive house plants. You won't need to rob your own luxuriant potted plants when for small sums you can buy the colorful foliage that will add so much to the distinction of arrangements. In water, most of this foliage keeps for weeks

Buy small plants:	Buy foliage of
Begonia (many types)	Big-leaf philodendrons
Caladium	Boston fern
Chinese evergreen	Calla lily
Dieffenbachia	Croton
English ivy	Camellia
Geranium	Emerald and jade
Pandanus	Figs (ficus)
Peperomia	Galax
Sansevieria	Huckleberry
Tri-leaf wonder	Salal (lemon leaves)
Wandering-jew	Scotch broom

Get to know broad-leaved evergreens

If you live in a climate where the broad-leaved evergreens thrive, you're in a flower arranger's paradise. Their handsome leaves combine so well with flowers that they're exciting to use. And they're also attractive in arrangements of foliage only. If these shrubs don't grow where you live, ask your florist to order the cut foliage of:

Bold-foliage types:	Delicate foliage
Banana-shrub	Boxorange
Camellia	Boxwood
Chinese photinia	Carolina laurel cherry
Common oleander	Evergreen euonymous
Glossy (wax-leaf privet)	Firethorn
	Jasmine
Japanese photinia	Nandina
Leatherleaf viburnum	Russian olive
Loquat	Southern waxmyrtle
Oregon hollygrape	Texas silverleaf
Pittosporum	True myrtle
Rhododendron	True lavender

Graceful ferns add so much to flowers

Many gardeners transplant hardy ferns from their wild habitats to cultivated gardens. Or you can buy sturdy roots of most ferns from your nurseryman. All ferns have in common a gracefulness and beauty of foliage that makes them ideal to use in flower arranging. Grow ferns, use them to add a luxury look to simplest of flowers

Beechfern	Male fern
Bracken, eastern	Ostrich fern
Cinnamon fern	Rattlesnake fern
Christmas fern	Royal fern
Ground cedar	Sensitive fern
Interrupted fern	Spleenwort, ebony
Lady fern, northern	Walking fern
Maidenhair fern	Woodfern, evergreen

foliage you should know

Needled evergreens good all year long

Evergreens are universal symbols of the holidays, but largely overlooked as additions to flower arrangements at other seasons of the year. Nearly all types we list grow in scores if not hundreds of varieties. If you have prized garden specimens, save clippings when you prune. Others grow freely along roadsides. Search for them when you go on a trip. They'll keep fresh in water for a long time

Arborvitae...flat, lacy, fernlike branches with leaf scales that overlap in irregular pattern. Colors vary from vivid green to gold

Fir..........looks much like spruce but its needles are soft and blunt. Some varieties are nearly silver, others are rich, dark green

Hemlock.....branches grow gracefully with flowing pendulous lines. Cones borne on twig ends. Widely used in Traditional arranging

Junipers.....new foliage is sharp, prickly; adult foliage is soft, scale-like. Much used in Oriental arranging; is easy to manipulate

Pine........is probably the most widely available evergreen. Choose one of its many varieties when you need really big branches

Spruce......needles are arranged all around twigs, giving branches a bushy look. Varieties come in many shades from gray to dark green

Yew.........flat, black-green needles have a shiny, leathery look; undersides are pale green. Suited to use as background for flowers

Use vine clippings for flowing effects

Readily available to home gardeners, but all too seldom put into use by flower arrangers are clippings from vines. Use them to get flowing lines in informal arrangements. Most of those we list are annuals, and easy to grow. Plant where they'll climb on a wall or trellis; use the cuttings to supplement arrangements of either fruit or flowers

Balloonvine
Bittersweet
Boston ivy
Bougainvillea
Canary bird vine
Cardinal climber
Cathedral bells
Chilean jasmine
Clematis
Gourds
Honeysuckle

Hyacinth bean
Mock cucumber
Moonflower
Morning glory
Nasturtium
Scarlet runner bean
Sweetpeas
Trumpet vine
Wild grape
Wintercreeper
Wisteria

Dry these for your winter bouquets

Gather foliage and seed pods from plants you'll find growing in fields and woods. Dry them to use in winter arrangements. To name a few: dock and cattails, jimsonweed, rye, wheat, barley, wild artemisia, tall grasses of many sorts, mullein rosettes

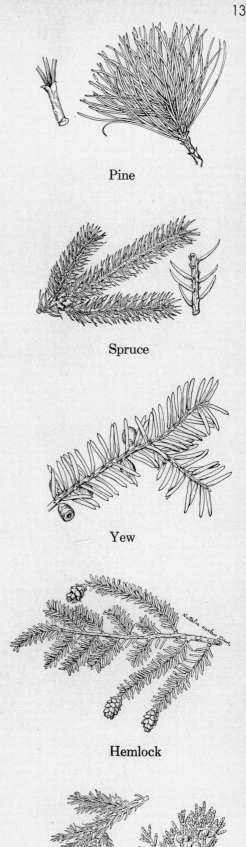

Pine

Spruce

Yew

Hemlock

Junipers

Chapter 4

Flowers make festive tables

Fresh flowers for the table! Just the phrase calls up a picture of hospitality, of food shared in a lighthearted mood, of pleasant occasions in the past when we have gathered, with family and friends, to enjoy one another's company in happy surroundings.

In the following pages we show you a wide variety of ways to use flowers and growing things as ornaments for festive tables. Some of the arrangements are formal; others are completely casual. But all—we trust—are designed to make the sharing of food a gracious occasion, not merely a concession to the human need to eat at regular intervals.

Centered table decorations

A symmetrical centerpiece, like the one of yellow roses across the page, is the usual choice when guests are to be seated at the sides of the table, host and hostess at the ends. Flowers used in this fashion should be equally attractive from all angles, and the centerpiece should be kept low enough so each diner can see all others without uncomfortable craning of necks.

Some arrangers insist that flower centerpieces be no taller than nine inches above table top. Such a rule is needlessly rigid. Feathery tufts, taller than this formula advocates, certainly wouldn't obstruct the view. So let this be the deciding factor when you are arranging flowers for the table, rather than demand a check with your ruler.

The color scheme's important

Think *color* first when you're selecting flowers for the table. They may match, harmonize, or contrast with colors of china, linens, or glassware and still create a delightful effect. But let it be clear that flower colors are part of a considered color scheme—not a happenstance matter.

Don't feel that everything must "match," but that it must "belong."

Yellow roses for a golden table-setting theme

Roses are secured on needlepoint holders in low crystal bowls set into a gold wire candelabra to form a symmetrical centerpiece. They're a perfect choice with a shimmering cloth, gold appointments

Pink and orchid set a tea table as romantic as an old-fashioned valentine. Quite in keeping is the old, fluted cranberry and milk-glass bowl holding 12 pink and white carnations, with lavender and white tuberoses placed to give height at center

Bud vase arrangement of spring flowers for bridge-luncheon is surrounded by four flower basket favors for the guests. Mixed pastel flowers are at their best when table settings are confined to one color only

Tables that welcome spring's return

Forsythia branches extend horizontal lines of a tulip-daffodil centerpiece

Set a spring party scene with just four daffodils, three tulips, and a half-dozen branch tips of forsythia. Let candles pick up yellow of the daffodils and forsythia blooms.

Footed bowl used as flower container ties in nicely with white dinnerware. Bowls needn't match but should be related to some other item used in a table setting. White pebbles conceal the needlepoint holder.

Create a spring landscape with branches of lilac, violets, and a bluebird

We owe Oriental flower arrangers a debt of gratitude for opening our eyes to the beauties of miniature re-created landscapes such as this one which fairly breathes of spring.

Lilac branches should be pruned to take wanted shapes, then secured on a sturdy needlepoint holder at one end of the shallow container.

Entire surface of water is covered with floating violets and their foliage to simulate an actual bed of violets blooming beneath a lilac bush.

Dainty decor for a bridge luncheon table

A few tulips, two leafy branches and a merry bluebird make a clever centerpiece for a luncheon served at the bridge table. Clear-glass container has been filled with green leaves to look like a grassy spot beneath flowers

Starched lace place mats establish theme of this table setting

Your choice of flowers for the table may be determined by any one of a number of things: the season, the occasion, room color scheme, china pattern, or—as here—by some detail such as the delicate tracery of starched lace place mats.

Clusters of lilac tips are secured on needlepoint holder in a low crystal saucer, almost completely disguised by flowers and leaves.

An added springtime touch are the dainty butterflies of wire and painted netting. Deftly handled, such details are real additions. If you are in doubt over suitability of accessories, omit them.

In a spirit of fun, let the Easter rabbit present your fresh springtime arrangement

Basket container and pink glass bunny say that this arrangement's intended to brighten a party for the young—in heart or years—during the Easter season.

For this arrangement, cut five flowering crab branches of various lengths and anchor at rear of large needlepoint holder, as a background for tulips. When using flowers of two colors in one group, be sure to put several flowers of like color close to each other. Random scattering gives a patchwork look. Place tallest tulips at the back and sides; short ones center and front.

A very tall arrangement like this one may be used on a table if placed at one end, but of course is unsuitable as a centerpiece. It would also be attractive on a buffet—if you are serving a meal in that style—with a similar but lower arrangement used on the table where guests are to be seated for eating.

Put summer's ornaments on party tables

*Table arrangement keyed to a casual
summer meal on a cool and shady porch*

Glass-top table in a frosty blue inspired this freely
flowing table arrangement in shades of pink, magenta,
and purple. Clipped from a summer border, it includes
zinnias, phlox, rosy loosestrife, and trailing stems of
petunias. Create your own "gardener's choice" arrangement to imitate summer's generous temperament

Easy-to-arrange centerpiece of asters and single mums
has charm but no pretensions. It's unconventional in
its mixture of flowers and colors, but calculated to add
warmth to an otherwise cool-color ensemble. Simple
way to make an arrangement of this kind is to cover a
low bowl with hardware cloth; insert flowers in holes

*Warm weather calls for easy
informality in your table settings*

Center gladiolus florets with rosebuds and cluster
them together to form a boutonniere of right size
for your silver comports. Shape a collar of green
leaves beneath each nosegay to give it a finished
look. Use the pair on a luncheon table; put silver
candelabra with them when it's a dinner party

Variation on a theme: instead of centering your
flowers and flanking them with candles, group the
candlesticks in middle of table and arrange the
flowers at each end. It's an attractive way to
use short-stemmed garden roses. Insert stems in
cupholders; hide mechanics with the rose leaves

Splash autumn's gold on tables in the

Add new importance to garden mums
with a "giant" from the greenhouse

Flaunt the stirring colors of Indian summer across your table with a trio of grouped bouquets of garden chrysanthemums in a long, metal container. Big, shaggy mum in center brings variety and a luxury look to arrangement

harvest spirit

Decorate fall social occasions with autumn's richly colored offerings

When fall's first crisp days put you in a mood to entertain, use the season's bounties for centerpieces that look like autumn.

Chrysanthemums, in their finest tawny tones, are the traditional flower of this time of the year. Use them often to crown a festive occasion. Vary the style of your arrangement and the type of mum you select to suit the degree of formality or informality of the party you are giving.

Don't overlook the pleasures of creating some of your centerpieces out of gleanings from your vegetable garden, such as small gourds and squash. They're a "natural" to blend with berried branches, fall leaves and grasses for informal table decorations.

Hawthorn branches, bearing their autumn-red fruits, are an interesting foil for a cluster of amusing little painted gourds. Basket container keeps to the informal character of the arrangement. Insert branches in heavy needlepoint cupholder that will take water to keep leaves fresh. Pile gourds around to disguise. Nice extra touch — if you grow your own gourds — is a clipping from the gourd vine, allowed to trail across table

Here's a new and fashionable trick you can use to brighten your luncheon or supper table: use napkins in a color that contrasts sharply with the cloth; then emphasize the contrast with flowers to match napkins. Three little bowls (you could use saucedishes from your set of china) of single yellow mums march down the center of the table informally. In this style of arrangement you can use only short-stemmed flowers, yet make a centerpiece that's suitable for long tables

Six ways to dress up wintertime festivities

Simple yet sophisticated use of evergreen tips and cones

Once you've devised so distinctive a color theme as this is in green, chartreuse, gold, and brown, stick to it in planning your centerpiece. A few spruce tips and three large pine cones painted chartreuse are in pleasing harmony with the setting

Flowers, ferns, candles form unit

Multicolor candles are not just an "extra" but are worked into the basic design of a simple centerpiece of roses and ferns which livens up this black and white table setting

Ebony base is part of the design

Casual centerpiece suits the easy informality of a breakfast table setting. Driftwood is decorated by daisies arranged on needlepoint holders set into catsup-bottle tops

Perfect as a buffet flower piece where you want some height are roses in a footed silver bowl, given a fanlike background with branches of fresh pine. It's a nice way to get extra mileage from silver serving dishes

Focus attention on an unusual candelabra by the addition of a few flowers and sprigs of foliage. (We used huckleberry here.) Arrange flowers and foliage so they will conceal the small cupholder into which they've been set

When your table setting and centerpiece are keyed to each other, both are enhanced

Unity of effect prevails when flowers and the manner in which they're arranged are in tune with the style and color of their setting.

Here, bird-of-paradise blooms and ti leaves arranged in a shallow, black bowl are good companions for a china patterned in bold, brilliant color.

Line arrangement as tall as this one may be used for a dining table when it's placed at one end. You could use the same flowers as a centerpiece if you cut them lower, so that height of arrangement does not interfere with cross-table view and conversation.

When you use a low flower bowl on a dining table, remember that the mechanics of the arrangement will be seen and will detract from the effect unless care is taken to conceal needle-point holder. Use foliage or—as here —attractive pebbles to hide holder and improve your total composition.

Flowers that make a buffet supper really special

Flowers will lend a gala atmosphere to the simplest buffet supper and send guests off remembering it as a really special affair.

You'll get the most dramatic effects if there's a relation between flowers used on table and buffet, and if both are keyed to color and style of their setting.

Next time you're planning a buffet-style supper party, establish a mood of expansive hospitality with flowers. Let them tell all your guests how glad you are that they came.

← As an ingenious way of displaying your roses, arrange them inside a pair of hurricane-style candleholders. Make sure rose foliage hides the cupholders in which you've inserted stem ends

Centerpiece of red roses with green and white accents glows against a pink cloth

Single-color schemes that use two or more shades of one hue are an almost sure-fire way to obtain a dramatic effect, and pink with red has real appeal.

White snaps and green foliage additions to the red roses introduce just enough contrast so the monochromatic treatment doesn't seem contrived or overdone.

Notice that tall red tapers exactly match the roses. It is attention to details of this sort which makes the difference between a table to remember as outstanding, and one which just misses true distinction.

Roses in hurricane-lamp candelabra will have guests saluting your ingenuity as a flower arranger. They take up little room on the buffet, but add greatly to the "it's a special occasion" air you're seeking. If you borrow this idea, relate the buffet and the table arrangements by using same flowers for both of them

A fine old epergne makes a lovely showcase for displaying the garden's finest blooms

If you use your dining-room table instead of a buffet when you give a "help yourself" style of supper party, a tall and stately epergne would make a magnificent centerpiece.

Here the spotlight is on rosy camellias, but many other flowers would be equally as impressive if shown in a similar fashion. Among those you might use instead are: fully open roses, tuberous begonias, carnations, dahlias.

The only important restriction on the kind of flowers you place in such an heirloom piece as this concerns quality. Flowers ought to be as fine as their container. The coarser garden flowers—good in sturdy ceramic containers—would be out of place in such elegant surroundings.

Accents for feminine table settings

Trim a luncheon table with this arrangement at one end, and its twin at the other. Three plaster canaries seem to perch on blossoming tips of crab. Tops of catsup bottles serve as cupholders for the ends of the branches. Foliage hides the bottle tops

Indulge your love of the dainty when you're setting your table for social gatherings of women friends

When your party is for ladies only, be as feminine as you please with flowers that will make the occasion a charming one. It's your chance to use all the ideas you've had to reject as too frilly for affairs that included men as well as women.

Let soft pastel shades, nosegay arrangements, and dainty accents be the order of the day. Your women guests will be flattered, and you'll have fun with an occasional splurge of femininity.

If one word of caution is not out of order in a discussion of feminine table settings, perhaps it should be said that accessories are best when used with some restraint. Don't scatter little figurines about your table. Work them into a flower arrangement *if* you can do it cleverly. Otherwise, omit!

Low bouquets looking like nosegays are easy to make with short-stemmed roses

If you're giving a party in honor of a bride-to-be, here's a clever idea for your flower arrangements.

Shaped to remind us of bridesmaids' bouquets, these nosegays of yellow rosebuds are perfectly suited to the pair of silver comports that are used as containers.

Arrangements of this kind may be made in the hand, using fine florists' wire to wrap the base and hold each flower in position. Or, you can assemble the bouquets on needlepoint holders, in the usual fashion. In either case, shape a collar of green leaves to give a finished look to the diminutive bouquets.

Central portion of each nosegay adds a little height and is made of forget-me-nots, white stephanotis. Lily-of-the-valley would be a good substitute if it is more available.

Several small silver cups are spaced down the center of the table, each one holding flowering twigs of hawthorn

Lace-paper collar adds to an old-fashioned bouquet

French or Victorian nosegays with a collar fashioned from a lace-paper doily are easily made to fit any size container—from an eggcup to the inexpensive glass vase pictured here.

A generous-size one would be fine as a centerpiece on your dining-room table. For a luncheon that's to be served at card tables, reduce the proportions to suit the space.

Almost any mixture of flowers will do, though pastel color schemes are most suitable for this type bouquet.

Celebrate Valentine's Day with flowers

Golden canaries surrounded by pink roses

Express Valentine Day's romantic theme with two little glass canaries, looking like lovebirds, nestled in a bower of pink roses. There are 13 blooms in this arrangement, cut to different stem lengths and secured in two needlepoint holders. Slant each rose so the head tips up to imitate the effectiveness of this design. Use some rose foliage to soften the stem lines, fill in the outline

Here's the way to arrange twelve red carnations in honor of St. Valentine

Heart-red carnations look all the redder against white of milk-glass epergnette that's used as the container for this bouquet.

It's an inexpensive and modern reproduction of an old-fashioned piece of hobnail glass, with Victorian airs that suit the sentimentality of St. Valentine's Day.

Carnations are by nature a somewhat stiff flower—a fact it's well to recognize in arranging them. Use care to cut stems to differing lengths; place so some will curve gracefully. Don't let all of them stand up straight, like so many soldiers lined up for review.

An arrangement of this kind is intended to be seen from three sides. Vary it a bit if you want to use as a table centerpiece so all views will be equally attractive. Or use it as it is, at one end of the table, or on the buffet.

*Decorate a teacup and saucer with
red hearts to hold seven fresh roses*

The unexpected container for this simple arrangement of seven red roses is what gives charm and a different air to an unsophisticated bouquet.

Our teacup and saucer came imprinted with the hearts—imported from Portugal—but any ordinary white cup and saucer could be made to look almost the same by decorating with paste-on hearts.

Saucer stands on a rack behind the teacup, and a black base gives the composition a finished look.

*Heart motif is carried out with
a white wire footed base for roses*

A bunch of short-stemmed pink roses is arranged in a green needlepoint cupholder, with a bud on top, largest blooms low in the design.

Completed arrangement is then set on a heart-shaped white wire base, to carry out a Valentine theme and supply a frame for the flowers.

Good substitute for this wire base would be a heart-shaped doily of lace paper, mounted on cardboard cut to the appropriate size. To add height, you could slip any small base underneath.

*Yellow roses with fern fronds
in a wreath of cardboard hearts*

Here's a clever centerpiece for a Valentine dinner or luncheon party. Ring of red cardboard hearts, pink cardboard bows wreathes an informal arrangement of roses and Boston fern fronds. Vary length of ferns according to size of your table. Centerpiece shouldn't be longer than one-third of table length

Tables set
to spread joy
at Eastertide

*A carpet of flowers under
a make-believe Easter-egg tree*

Like a woodsy carpet of flowers, a cluster of mixed spring blooms is arranged in a hidden needlepoint cupholder, then set onto a polished burl base.

Also secured in the holder is a stark branch bearing Easter eggs of gay tints.

Duplicate this whimsical arrangement to liven up any Eastertime party table.

*A handful of spring
blooms brings warmth to
table set with milk glass*

Stark white milk glass responds to the warmth and color of some informally grouped spring-flowering branches and blooms that decorate a table set for an Easter breakfast or luncheon.

The three flower containers do not exactly match the tableware but are also of milk glass and so blend nicely. All pieces are of modern make and inexpensive.

Small needlepoint holders secure the several varieties of early tulips and narcissus in the small bowls. In the taller container, some trailing sprays of flowering almond accompany a few big and brightly colored tulips.

As an added party note, drop a sprig of flowering almond onto the plate of each of your guests.

Flowery background for a china Easter egg

If you have among your treasures a delicately decorated china Easter egg, let everyone enjoy it on your party table. Here we've given it an airy background of white lilac and tulips. Around its base, lilac foliage, and colorful candy Easter eggs form a decorative wreath

Plan a royal spring color scheme around violets, tulips, and tinted eggs

Bunches of fresh violets—a sure sign of spring—mingle with pink and gold tulips in this view-from-all-sides centerpiece. Crumpled chicken wire in a shallow baking dish, or a large posy ring, will hold short-stemmed flowers like these in place.

You can make a bunny silhouette similar to this one if you're handy with wire and a soldering iron. Tint the eggs in rainbow hues to blend with flowers.

A basket of lilacs and tulips to brighten an Easter breakfast table

If your family looks on Easter breakfast as a special occasion, pay tribute to the joyful gathering with a centerpiece of the freshest of spring's flowers.

Fragrant lilacs and brilliant tulips are a treat for both eye and nose that will put everyone in the proper mood to enjoy the food about to be eaten together.

A pale yellow straw basket is the container we chose as appropriate to the informal meal.

We allowed some of the lilacs to nod against the basket handles, others to spill out beyond its edges in a free-and-easy arrangement anyone could duplicate. A concealed bowl supplies water.

Fruits and flowers spell Thanksgiving

Spill green grapes lavishly forth from a straw cornucopia

Pale green grapes, generously cascading out of a simple straw cornucopia, look twice as luscious for their deep purple background. If your cloth is a green one, reverse the scheme and use purple grapes to get a similar effect. Add a few grape leaves—real or artificial—as a nice supplement to grapes, and for color contrast

Gleam of candles and glow of gold add sophistication to a centerpiece of mixed fruits

Centerpieces of fruit are never more thoroughly in keeping with the occasion than upon our Thanksgiving dinner tables. The bounty of fall, in the form of ripe fruits, reminds us of the reason for the first American Thanksgiving, when our Pilgrim forefathers expressed thanks for a rich harvest season which had just ended.

This bowl and candelabra are one unit, but you could use a separate fruit dish and candelabra similarly on your Thanksgiving table, at one end, or—if they're kept low— as a centerpiece. Let grapes flow over edges, and fill in the bare spots.

Arrangements of fruit always have greater effectiveness if you concentrate on relatively few colors; don't use some haphazard mixture which appears to be unplanned.

Thanksgiving dinner's just the right occasion to center your table arrangement around a handsome "decoy." Pine branches, garden mums and colored autumn leaves are secured invisibly on needlepoint holders in glass cups around edge of duck. Choose the mum colors that will contrast or harmonize best with your tablecloth

Treasured silver shows off the season's harvest of fruits in regal style

Here's evidence that a centerpiece of fruit can be equal to the most elegant of table settings. Arranged in a beautiful old silver fruit basket, there's a richness about the grouping which matches fine linen, crystal and silver used with it.

In Colonial days, no flowers were ever used to decorate dining tables—only fruits. You'll be in the spirit of the first Thanksgiving if you choose to have a centerpiece of fruit.

Cut flowers for fresh Christmas beauty

Perch a cascade of carnations and holly atop an elegant silver candelabra

Brilliant companion for fine silver is a burst of red carnations, spilling over sprigs of variegated holly. A glass bowl holding water for flowers and foliage is anchored to central candleholder with a sticker disc from jeweler. Display this arrangement on tea or buffet table and add to effect with clusters of carnations, holly on tea tray

Roses and greens between two angels

Demure ceramic angels, each holding a slim red taper, are placed at either end of an arrangement of red roses, against a cool sweep of greens, in a low, white ceramic bowl.

Small lamb nestles in greens placed to unify the arrangement and accompanying figurines.

Grouping like this is good either as a table centerpiece or a mantel decoration. If used on table, keep greens low enough to see across.

Snowy centerpiece for a card table

When Christmas dinner is buffet style, and guests are eating at card tables, put compact centerpieces on each. Plastic-foam base is centered with snow-sprayed chicken-wire cone. Roses, holly get water supply from florists' tubes or from nonspillable water. Insert the greens, tree balls in the plastic base

Combine poinsettias and evergreen

Evergreen branches give height to low arrangement of three poinsettia blooms in shallow bowl. Set it on a coffee or end table, or on a buffet.

Prepare poinsettia stems first by removing lower leaves, then searing with candle each place where a leaf was removed. Also sear cut end until milky sap stops flowing. Soak stems in water before arranging.

It's a Merry Christmas breakfast table

Set a basketful of flowers on the breakfast table to heighten that delightful Christmas morning mood. Key the flower colors to table setting, as has been done here, with red, green, white, and yellow of blooms and foliage repeated in cloth, china, and egg-cup decorations. Put a glass bowl inside the basket to hold a needlepoint and supply water for the flowers, foliage

Chapter 5

Here's what it takes to win a prize

To create beauty, and to share with others one's personal grasp of its nature are the twin forces that motivate all true artists, including flower arrangers. Flower-show entries carried out in this spirit will enrich both the arranger and the viewer.

For the stimulus they have provided to so many women to create and to receive pleasure from viewing the tasteful flower designs of others, much credit is due the State Garden Clubs and their National Council. They have set standards of excellence for staging, exhibiting, and judging flower shows that are universally followed and respected.

Examine the show schedule

If you want to enter an arrangement in a flower show, your first step is to secure a copy of the schedule and study it carefully. Select a class whose specifications are a challenge to your imagination. Then decide on the particular materials you will use.

Make several practice arrangements, trying each time to improve, until you feel you've accomplished the most artistic flower design that you are capable of executing.

Follow rules conscientiously

Pay especial attention to the stated limitations on kinds of plant materials, as well as accessories, colors, containers, and backgrounds you are asked to use.

Take note of space allotments and design your arrangement in the proper scale—not too large or too small. If a niche or shadow box is specified, take that into account in creating your flower design.

Study prizewinners pictured

On the facing and following pages we include pictures of prizewinning arrangements (and more tips on entering shows). Study them for help in creating designs that win.

Blue ribbon was won in the "Return to Tradition" class by this mass arrangement. Designed by the Libertyville (Illinois) Town and Country Garden Club. Footed bowl complements style of bouquet

Roses of delicate pink, carnations of a deeper tone, with a background of iris and funkia foliage were used in this arrangement. It took a blue ribbon in the "Party Pink" class. Designed by Mrs. Jack Rardin, Akron, Ohio

Creative way to use foliage

First prize in "A Touch of Genius" class was awarded to this all-foliage arrangement. It was designed by the Riverside (Illinois) Garden Club.

Foliage included in the design: salal, variegated pittosporum, and some rosettes fashioned of galax leaves, placed at center front of the arrangement.

The folding screen that serves as background for the composition was covered in a watered silk of a pale hue. It supplies interesting contrasts of both color and texture to those of the foliage.

Arrangements may include sculpture as well as flowers

Many arrangers—particularly those to whom the Modern style of flower arranging is most congenial—often include sculpture in their arrangements. They may do this to advance a theme, to set a mood, or simply as an extra challenge to their skill at designing.

When to use sculpture

If you are entering a flower show, you will, of course, include a piece of sculpture, a statuette, or a figurine *only* if it is permitted by the specifications of the class in which you're entering an arrangement.

In addition, you should be certain that it has intrinsic merit of its own. If it is of poor quality, it can only detract from the total effect of beauty you wish to create.

Avoid these mistakes

There are some common mistakes made by entrants in flower shows that will immediately disqualify their arrangements, no matter how artistic or attractive they may be. You can avoid most of them by a careful reading of the schedule, and strict adherence to the specifications it lists.

Here's a sampling of "don'ts" to remember as you prepare your entry: if the schedule calls for six varieties of Darwin tulips, it won't do to slip in a few early flowering ones for variety; when it says you may use just 12 daffodils, it is not acceptable to add an extra one or two which you happen to have left over; should it request a collection of annuals only, don't insert branches of flowering shrubs to improve your design.

Conceal the mechanical aids

No matter what the style of the arrangement you're entering, avoid permitting the mechanical aids to show. Wire, needlepoint holders, tape, and the like are essential to many of the most interesting flower designs, but they should remain hidden from view.

Interpret a classical theme

Goddess Diana is set against gladiolus stems with unopened buds and broad canna leaves for contrast. Echeveria rosettes are placed low, at sides. Two rectangles of white marble form appropriate base. Designed by Mrs. Henry Haas, it won blue ribbon at Akron Garden Forum

Polished wood base unifies figurine and rose arrangement

Pink roses, brown beech leaves, dock, and a gracefully curved bare branch make a tranquil, natural scene for the admiration of a gentle St. Francis, with the traditional birds at his feet.

Roses and statuette would not be so well related if they were not both placed on polished burl base.

This arrangement, by Mrs. A. B. Arrington, won a blue ribbon at the Akron, Ohio, Rose Show.

Exotic figurine is in harmony with design of ti leaves and orchids

"Sculptured Elegance" was the title of the class in which this arrangement won a first prize. The three cylindrical containers holding plant materials were covered in the brown fabric which also forms a base for the grouping as a whole.

Small figurine is of dark, brown wood. Ti leaves are green; orchids shade from green to brown. Designed by the Garden Club of Lincolnwood, Illinois.

Tell the story of spring

The class in which this arrangement was awarded a blue ribbon was entitled "Memo to Moderns." It was designed by the Maywood (Illinois) Garden Club and includes black statuette, budding branch, grouping of blooms of spring-flowering bulbs. The zebra-striped fabric at right was part of design

Originality is one of the goals

Inspiration to use familiar materials in new ways is one of the valuable contributions a flower show makes to arrangers and viewers.

If you've gone along for years making more or less the same arrangements of roses, carnations, or whatever your favorite flowers may be, attend a flower show and come away with ideas on exciting new treatments of old, familiar flower friends of yours.

Better yet, *enter* a flower show and let the specifications for one of the classes stimulate you to renewed creativity.

The floral designs pictured on these pages include few exotic plant materials. But each has an air of originality because of the way

flowers are assembled, an unusual container, or the kinds of accessories used. And each is a result of some inventive and creative thinking on the part of the designer.

When showtime arrives

Know exactly when you're expected to have your arrangement in place. Arrive with all the supplies you need and complete your arrangement promptly. Accompany it with the proper entry card, correctly filled in.

Finally, relax and rest assured that if you took pleasure in creating a design, you have had your reward, whether you win or not.

Designed of autumn's fruits

Curving sprays of high-bush cranberry are centered with cluster of cherry bell tomatoes. Unusual container is wine bottle imported from South America. It comes in an interestingly woven raffia cover. Designed by Mrs. Merrill Cook, this arrangement won a blue ribbon in the Des Moines (Iowa) Garden Club's autumn flower show

Yellow roses in a sophisticated curving line

Pale yellow roses, stripped of foliage, stems manipulated to assume an interesting line effect, took first prize in class titled "Sleek Sophistication." The outsize green glass goblet and white marble base add to the over-all dramatic effect of the arrangement. This floral design was created by the Oak Lawn (Illinois) Garden Club

Lilies treated with simplicity

This arrangement of Madonna lilies and funkia foliage was awarded a blue ribbon in a class stressing fragrance, part of Fifth District summer show of Iowa Federation of Garden Clubs. Low container maintains a mood of simplicity established by the arrangement. The designer is Mrs. F. W. Pickworth

Spring fashion commentary

Milliner's hat display form of woven wicker encloses red carnations; more carnations peek out at the top and bottom. Background of black velvet and checked fabric are part of the design. Created by the Elgin (Illinois) House and Garden Club, it won first in the "Dior Dictates" class

Nature scene uses dried materials

Mojave wood forms the line, and yellow yarrow, treated brown beech leaves, dock are the mass in this blue-ribbon arrangement by Mrs. A. B. Arrington, entered in Garden Forum of Greater Akron (Ohio). Ducks are of brown wood; bills and feet yellow. Plaque is walnut

Calla lilies in a crescent shape

Calla lilies and self-foliage are displayed in a black urn, against a black velvet drapery, in triptych covered with metallic fabric. Entered in "Dache's Choice" class, the arrangement won a first for the Garden Club of Skokie (Illinois)

Index